TABLE OF CONTENTS

ILLUSTRATIONS

CHAPTER 1

INTRODUCTION

> Genuine negotiations will not be easy. I found this out the hard way. But Somalis must consider the alternative: the violence will continue and the rest of the world will continue to use land as a playground for intervention.[1]
> —Nuruddin Farah, *My Life as a Diplomat*

Creating a functioning state in Somalia means negotiation, reconciliation and sharing of power among Somalis. Yet in the last 20 years "genuine negotiations" did not occur. International attempts at solving Somalia's instability resulted in the establishment of central governments that barely exerted control over a few square miles. These transitional governments lacked legitimacy, and even worse, hurt the Somali people through corruption and theft.

This thesis argues that internal Somali politics primarily causes Somalia's problems. Ending the mass atrocities occurring in Somalia entails building national unity and sharing power across individuals, clans and rivals. Compromise will lead to a responsive government able to feed its people, secure its borders and combat terrorists on its own. However, the difficulty lies in removing those who benefit from the current system so that power devolves to the people. Only Somalis can create lasting change by building trust between different factions who will in turn demand good governance and different leaders.

Imposing an international solution or backing foreign participation in power-brokering agreements will backfire in countries like Somalia without a history of central government or sense of statehood. Nation building in a country where its citizens do not agree concerning basics such as borders, citizenship and constitutional structure will fail since there exists no indigenous center or ideology to force competing groups to compromise. Therefore, the international community, if it intervenes, should promote programs and organizations that support Somali-led reconciliation. The world community can assist by offering support to burgeoning members of civil society and by ensuring Somalia's national resources go towards the Somali people.

For over 20 years Somalia endured turmoil caused by militia warfare, corruption and terrorism. Somalis suffered because of the governing dysfunction. Hundreds of thousands died, millions emigrated or fled to refugee camps; and violence, especially against Somali women and girls, reached unparalleled levels (see chapter 5). Indeed, Genocide Watch regularly places Somalia on its watch list for crimes committed by the Islamic fundamentalist group, Harakaat al-Shabaab al-Mujaahidiin, commonly known as Al-Shabaab or "Movement of Warrior Youth." These crimes against other Somalis include rape, abduction of children as soldiers and murder.[2] Moreover, some have argued that the Somali transitional government committed crimes against humanity through its misappropriation of foreign aid.[3] In summary, a lack of governance left Somalia as the quintessential failed state; an ongoing humanitarian disaster, a sanctuary for pirates and a terrorist threat to the world community.

As a failed state located in a strategic area, Somalia attracted international interventions and protracted discussion. Its collapse engendered debate concerning the cause of its dysfunction and what should be done to establish stability. The most common reasons given for Somalia's failure include: its clan system, enduring effects of colonialism, lack of sufficient economic recourses, and blundering by the international community at peace building. While these factors play a role in explaining Somalia's collapse, they do not reach the heart of the problem.

Lack of international attention did not cause Somalia's instability. The US and the international community attempted every avenue of influence from diplomatic, information, economic and military means to achieve peace. Since 1995, the international community has hosted over 15 peace conferences. The Arab League, European Union, African Union, Intergovernmental Authority on Development and individual nations such as Turkey and the United Arab Emirates all have engaged Somalia and offered developmental assistance. Indeed, two international conferences have already been held in 2012, one in the United Arab Emirates and the other in London. Currently, the United Nations (UN) has sixteen agencies in Mogadishu to implement stabilization and recovery efforts.[4]

Economically, since 1991 the international community provided Somalia with approximately $13 billion in financial aid.[5] Militarily, in 1992 the US sent 37,000 troops to Somalia in Operation Restore Hope and the UN later authorized 28,000 troops for its mission. In 2007 the UN approved the African Union Mission in Somalia (AMISOM) to support reconciliation efforts. In February 2012, the UN Security Council approved increasing AMISOM in Somalia forces to 17,731 troops to fight Al-Shabaab and support Somalia's transitional government.[6] In 2011 Ethiopian and Kenyan troops entered Somalia to also combat Al-Shaabab. However, even this level of military intervention and economic support has not produced stability or a functioning government.

By the same token, Somalia's failure has not been caused by clan rivalry in and of itself. While clan identity plays a vital role in Somali society, organization and culture, the existence of clan structure did not cause this level of turmoil; rather the exploitation of clan identity caused conflict. For example, when General Said Barre overthrew the democratically elected Somali government in 1969, he outlawed the influence of clan politics in government. But when his government began to topple in the late 1980s, Barre exploited clan rivalries to maintain power (see chapter 2). The ensuing "winner-take-all" ethos of rivaling clans dominated the political environment since.

Economic need does not explain Somalia's instability either. Somalia may be one of the poorest countries in the world, but Somali entrepreneurs succeed in Somalia and across the globe. Somalia has some of the least expensive and best cell phone service in Africa. Members of the Somali diaspora transfer around $1 billion in remittances each year to Somalia using the *hawala,* or trust-based money transfer system.[7] Somali businesses continue to function often without essential government services such as electricity and running water. Somali immigrants across Kenya and South Africa established profitable businesses. Throughout Africa Somalis are renown for establishing a profitable business where no one has before.[8]

Lack of a functioning government, rather than the above reasons, underlies Somalia's problems. The Somali transitional government cannot meet its minimum governing obligations to provide basic security and essential services to its people. The Transitional Federal Government (TFG) in place since 2004 completed none of its targeted tasks, except keeping itself in existence. In June 2011 the TFG extended its mandate for another year, yet this year-long extension occurred after the international community convinced the TFG to reduce the extension from the three years it originally proposed. Later that year the TFG, regional provincial governments and the UN agreed to an End of the Transition Roadmap with a timetable for the TFG to draft a Constitution and hold national elections by August 2012. Roadmap meetings have been held, but signs pointing to Somali resolve have not been promising. The intractability of business-as-usual politics has been demonstrated by violent fist-fights within the Somali Parliament, by the proposed four-year implementation delay agreed to during December talks at Garowe, and the widespread belief that citizens and their true representatives have not been consulted on the draft Constitution.[9]

Notwithstanding political intransience, military forces have made impressive gains. African Union troops along with troops from neighboring countries have put Al-Shabaab on the run. The TFG controls most of Mogadishu for the first time in years. Al-Shabaab lost strongholds near the Ethiopia and Kenya borders. With Al-Shabaab losing ground and popular support, the prospects of peace grow high. This year presents a promising opportunity for Somalia to reclaim its future. However given the level of dysfunction in Somalia, international assistance may be needed to establish accountable governance. This assistance should be tailored to Somalia's specific culture and history and would entail a less direct approach.

<u>Momentum to Intervene</u>

While pulling back from Somalia and allowing Somalis to solve their own problems may be a tempting solution, the geopolitical importance of Somalia renders a complete hands-off approach untenable. Al-Shabaab acts across the East African region and pirates continue to plague international trade routes. Disengaging or attempting to contain these actors from afar without going to the root of Somalia's instability will only decrease the ability of legitimate Somali society to function. In addition to countering security threats, actors from afar, without going to the root of Somalia's instability, will only decrease the the suffering of the Somali people. The world's agreement concerning the Responsibility to Protect demands international attention and assistance.

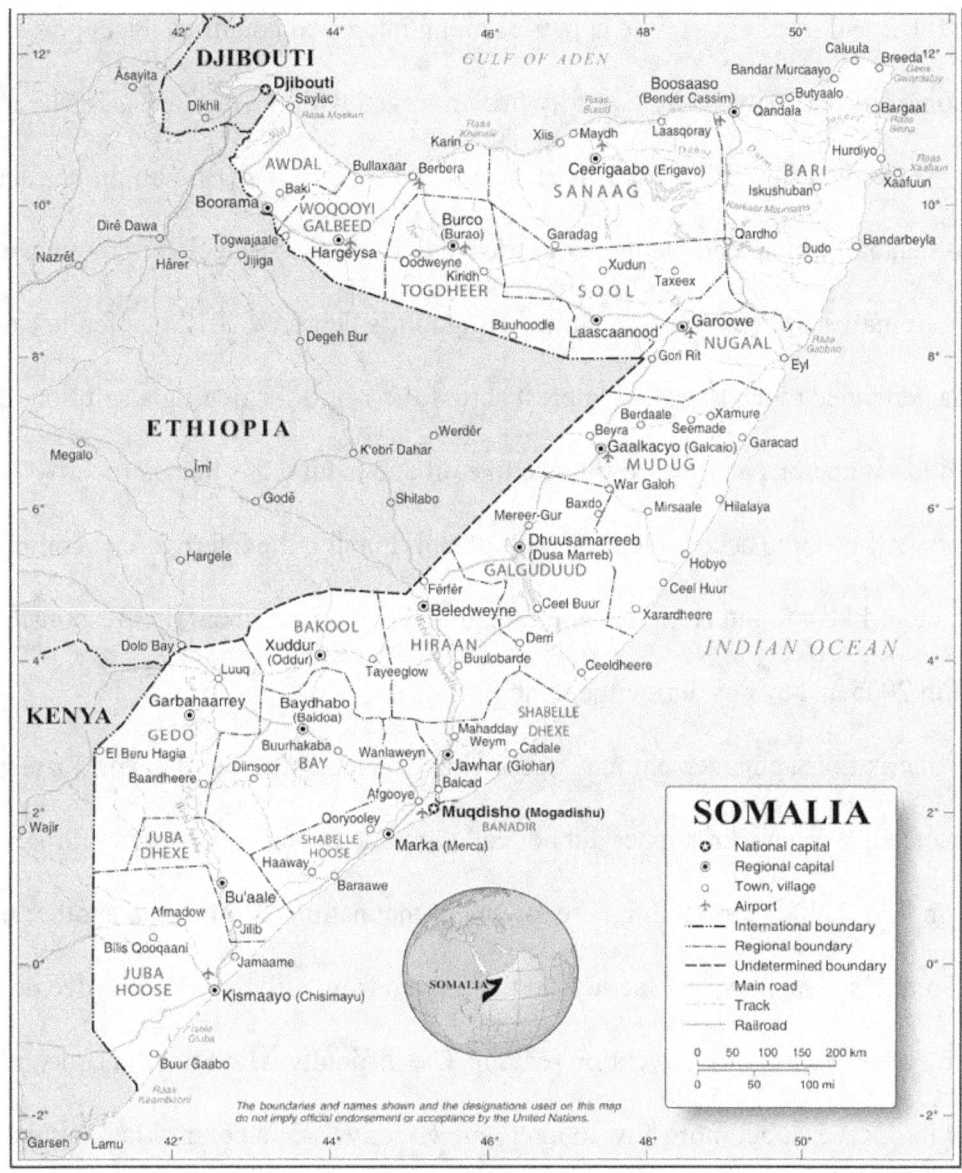

Figure 1. Map of Somalia with Officially Recognized Administrative Districts

The time may be right for the international community to intervene more decisively in Somalia. Numerous factors point to this conclusion. First, the attention of international leaders and the public has been focused on Somalia this year due to the 2011 famine and resulting humanitarian crisis. Second, the mandate for the TFG ends in August 2012 and there exists little appetite among interested countries to support another extension of its authority. Third, security has improved with the military gains by AMISOM, Kenyan and Ethiopian forces. Fourth, frustration with Somali pirates and fears that Al-Shaabab will spread to other countries underlines the strategic importance of creating Somali stability. Fifth, the United Kingdom's February 2012 Conference on Somalia generated much hope and interest across the world for finding a solution. Sixth, Somalia has numerous national resources, like oil and natural gas that as security improves will be more accessible for development. Finally, the international community may be more likely to intervene given international agreement about the Responsibility to Protect in 2005 and events during the Arab Spring.

International engagement may not always be successful, but the world's response has advanced. Warren Christopher did not call the issue of state-sponsored killing a "problem from hell"[10] for nothing. The argument that nations should stop another nation, or in Somalia's case, powerful factions in that nation from killing its own is decided, while the complexities of intervention remain. The difficulty with Somalia concerns less the will to intervene, but more how to intervene effectively in a country lacking the fundamentals of a modern state.

Research Question and Methodology

Somalia presents the question of what the world community should do when all traditional methods of humanitarian intervention have failed. How should the world respond to the ongoing famine, civil war and death occurring in Somalia when 20 years of intervention have failed and even potentially made the situation worse by reinforcing dependence on foreign assistance? Does the world have an interest in more than simply containing the destabilizing repercussions of Somalia, such as combating pirates and terrorists without addressing their root causes? If the international community does have an interest, should it intervene dramatically or follow the advice of many commentators who argue that the international community should provide financial assistance but disengage from a broader response? Advocates of the Somali-led process argue that top-down approaches have proven not to work and that Western notions of modern good governance do not take advantage of traditional Somali clan-based, elder dominated negotiations and Islamic traditions.

In summary, the primary question of this thesis is: What method of international intervention, if any, will create a stable and secure Somalia? Assuming any outside intervention would promote stability. The secondary question is: Should the international community lead the effort to establish stability in Somalia, or should the world community step back, provide financial assistance and guidance if asked, but allow Somalis to lead and structure the stabilization effort?

The last 20 years in Somalia present a case study of state dissolution and the myriad ways the international community has responded to a collapsed state. The research methodology for this study is qualitative. It analyzed numerous sources to

8

address how the Somali government collapsed, why it continues to remain dysfunctional and what actions would make the country stable again. This study reviewed theories and methods on international intervention to stop a mass atrocity or genocide; case studies concerning previous interventions; and statements from governments and international institutions regarding humanitarian intervention. This study also reviewed literature concerning Somalia's modern history, economy, society and politics. The study reviewed documents from the UN, African Union, TFG, and U.S. government as well as newspaper articles, journal articles and blogs from Somali writers.

Review of Major Literary Resources

The literature reviewed fell under four main subject areas: theory and history of international intervention to confront a mass atrocity; modern history, culture and economy of Somalia; analysis of international interventions in Somalia' and review of literature concerning stabilization and reconstruction in failed states.

Samantha Powers in A *Problem from Hell,* describes how U.S. policy toward humanitarian intervention has been one of denial and inaction. Numerous individuals and organizations have written proposals on how to respond to mass atrocities or prevent them. These include the *Mass Atrocity Response Operations: A Military Planning Handbook (MARO Handbook),* and *Preventing Genocide: A Blueprint for U.S. Policymakers.* The *MARO Handbook* presents a planning framework, based on joint planning guidance on how the military could intervene during a mass atrocity. *Genocide Studies and Prevention*, the official Journal of the International Association of Genocide Scholars, dedicated its Spring 2011 issue to commentaries on the *MARO Handbook*. Comments concerning the *MARO Handbook* criticized its lack of historical context and superficiality, its militarization of the problem, lack of political discussion concerning when to intervene, simplistic analysis of the problems of intervention and questions concerning the true motivation for Western countries to intervene during a mass atrocity. A corollary to the *MARO Handbook, The Mass Atrocity Prevention Handbook,* provides methods for agencies across the U.S. government to intervene in a troubled country before mass killings occur.

Preventing Genocide: A Blueprint for U.S. Policymakers, by the Genocide Prevention Task Force outlines steps that the U.S. should take in order prevent genocide. The current administration has enacted some of the recommendations, including mentioning genocide prevention in the 2010 National Security Strategy and the Presidential Study Directive on Mass Atrocities.

Ioan Lewis has studied Somalia for the last 40 years and is the preeminent outside expert on Somali history and culture. *Understanding Somalia and Somaliland* discusses Somali clan system, pastoralism, Islamic tradition and fierce independence of the Somali people. Mark Bradbury, in *Becoming Somaliland,* discusses the history of Somaliland, why Somaliland is more stable than Somalia and the reasons why Somaliland so adamantly requests its independence from Somalia. In *Understanding the Somalia Conflagration: Identity, Political Islam and Peacebuilding,* Afyare Abdi Elmi, a Somali immigrant, conducted numerous interviews with Somalis concerning clan identity and Islamic beliefs. He also discusses Ethiopia's, and to a lesser extent, Kenya's attempts to destabilize Somalia.

Two other books place Somalia's political problems in the broader context of describing how a country establishes democratic rule, and thereby, is less likely to commit atrocities against its own people. Claude Ake, a Nigerian political scientist, analyzes failures of economic and political development in Africa in *The Feasibility of Democracy in Africa.* He describes how the ruling elite exploit their country's resources and peoples in a winner-takes-all struggle. In *Why Nations Fail,* Daron Acemoglu and Jams Robinson conduct a sweeping historical analysis of countries that prospered and those that failed. The difference concerns inclusive versus extractive governments.

Reports from the United Nations Monitoring Group on Somalia and Eritrea provide detailed analysis of terrorist groups operating in Somalia, corruption of the Somali government and piracy that threaten the peace and stability of the region. Testimony in front of the U.S. Congress provides insight into U.S. policy toward Somalia and the U.S. analysis of the reasons for Somalia's collapse.

Important literature for the thesis also includes review of blogs and articles written by Somalis. As Matt Baugh, the current Ambassador to Somalia from the United Kingdom, stated in his blog on the London Conference, "Somalis around the globe love political debate."[11] An Internet search of Somali commentary on present events demonstrates a sophisticated, historically focused analysis of politics and society.

---

[1]Nuruddin Farah,"My Life as a Diplomat," *The New York Times,* 26 May 2007. Mr. Farah is a Somali novelist who now lives in South Africa.

[2]Genocide Watch, "Mass Atrocities Alert: Somalia," March 2012, http://www.genocidewatch.org/somalia.html (accessed 5 April 2012), 4.

[3]Matt Bryden, "Somalia's Famine is Not Just a Catastrophe, It's a Crime," October 2011, http://www.enoughproject.org/files/Bryden_SomaliaFamine%20 Brief_final_0.pdf (accessed 3 May 2012).

[4]United Nations, *Special Report of the Secretary-General on Somalia*, 31 January 2012, 3.

[5]John Norris and Bronwyn Burton, "The Price of Somalia's Failure, How Much Has the Collapse of Somalia Cost the World?" *Foreign Policy,* 5 October 2011, http://www.foreignpolicy.com/articles/2011/10/05/the price of failure?(accessed 15 December 2011).

[6]United Nations, *United Nations Security Council Resolution 2036,* 22 February 2012.

[7]Tatiana Nenova and Tim Harford, "Anarchy and Invention: How Does Somalia's Private Sector Cope without Government," *Public Policy for the Private Sector* (Washington, DC: World Bank, November 2004), 3.

[8]See Kantai, Parselelo, and Patrick Smith, "The Dangers of Carving Up Somali," *The Africa Report,* 6 Febuary 2011, http://www.theafricareport.com/ index.php /news-analysis/the-dangers-of-carving-up-somalia-50180834.html (accessed 10 March 2012). "The tremendous success of Somali traders in Johannesburg, Cape Town and Nairobi's Eastleigh district points to the potential for the country's economy, if Somalia's people can find their own political solution as international pressure mounts."

[9]Mubarak, "Mubarak's Musings, Somalia's Roadmap to Peace or War?" *Somalia Report*, 2 May 2012, http://www.somaliareport.com/index.php/post/3306/ Mubaraks_Musings (accessed 3 May 2012).

[10]Samantha Power, *A Problem from Hell: America and the Age of Genocide* (New York: Basis Books, 2002), xiii.

[11]Matt Baugh, "London Conference on Somalia: Political Process," http://blogs.fco.gov.uk/mattbaugh/ (accessed 8 February 2012).

CHAPTER 2

SMASHING THE FIVE-POINTED STAR

Somalis, Bwana, they no good; each his own Sultan.[1]
    —Said Samatar, quoting advice given to British officer

On 1 July 1960, the Somali Republic was born. Previously, on 26 June 1960, British Somaliland gained independence from the United Kingdom. Four days later, Italian Somaliland, located to the southeast, received its independence from the Italian-administered UN trusteeship and on the same day merged with the former British protectorate to form the new country. The Somali Republic's founders envisioned a state that would encompass the entire Somali nation across East Africa. The five points of the Somali point to the regions where ethnic Somalis traditionally live: the two regions inside Somalia's borders, British Somaliland in the northwest and rest of Somalia to the east and south; and three regions outside of its border, Djibouti to the northwest, the Ogaden province of Ethiopia and the northeastern part of Kenya. However, the dream of uniting a "Greater Somalia" ended in 1978. The failure of the irredentist enterprise continues to influence Somalia today. It set the stage for Somalia's disintegration as a cohesive state and it left an ideological vacuum yet to be filled by a belief that will bind Somalis in a common national identity.

According to tradition, Somalis trace their lineage to a common Arab ancestor from whom sprang the current six major Somali clans: Darod, Dir, Digil and Mirifle, Hawiye, Rahanweyn and Isaaq.[2] For Somalis belonging to a clan identifies a person to others, defines a person's own identity, binds individuals together to support each other, especially in times of turmoil, and can be used for political or financial gain.[3] Clan

13

members intermarry, but base clan affiliation on patrilineal decent. Clans dominate certain geographical areas, for example the Issaq form the majority clan in Somaliland, and the Hawiye the majority in the area surrounding Mogadishu.

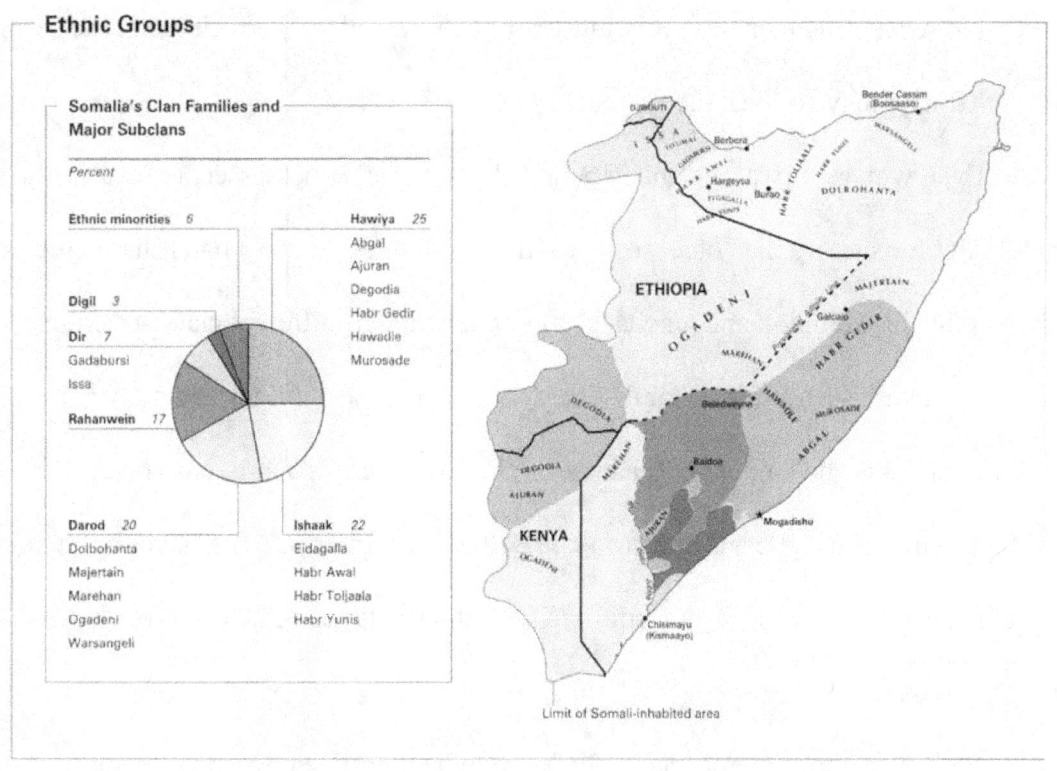

Clan identity remains a strong force in Somalia, lasting long after various attempts to suppress its influence. Clan membership decides representation in the TFG with a percentage of the assembly's seats going to major clans under the 4.5 rule where the four major clans receive a greater share of seats than the minority clans. Colloquial examples of the significance of clan affiliation abound. Afyare Elmi tells of postal instructions given to him by a Somali man in 2007. A package would be delivered to him if the delivery company was given his three names (first name, father's name and grandfather's name), his clan, sub-clan and the city where he lives.[4] In another example, a prominent Somali run aid organization that provides care to all Somalis made its first rule that to receive aid clan or family must not be discussed by the recipients. The second rule is that men may not beat their wives.[5]

Even with clan rivalries, many believed that Somalia possessed a greater opportunity for success than other former African colonies since Somalis shared the same culture, ethnicity, religion and language. Yet while similar, different class structures arose in Somali history with pastoralist herders on top of society. Immediately beneath them are farmers. The Digil and Rahanweyn clans grow crops and live in the agricultural area between the Shebelle and Juba rivers.[6] Below the farmers are the Jareer or "hard-haired" who are Somalised Bantu from pre-Somali populations or those brought to Somalia as slaves.[7]

Perhaps common egalitarian beliefs is a more significant reason to explain Somali's resistance to central government rather than differences among Somalis. European colonists coming into contact with Somalis described them as the "Irish of Africa" for their antiauthoritarian attitude.[8] Even today, nomadic pastoralists make up 60 to 70 percent of the population and their influence extends to Somalis living in urban areas who continue to hold economic interests in their relative's herds.[9] Scholars describe Somali society as egalitarian, segmentary and a "highly devolved, horizontally constructed, and decentralized society."[10] Somalis can be persuaded, but not told what to do. Traditional clan structure may have elders with persuasive authority and respect, but not chiefs.[11] Clan elders persuade through wisdom, experience and speaking ability. As a nation of poets, Somalis expect clan elders to speak engagingly for hours. This dispersed view of authority survives today. For example, while teaching in Somalia in the 1960s, the participants of a college curriculum meeting surprised an American professor. Not only did students, faculty and administrators attend the meeting, but cooks, drivers and janitors did as well. The cooks and drivers even made suggestions on changes to the curriculum, which surprised the American. However, none of the Somalis thought their participation strange since it reflected the lack of hierarchical structure in Somali society.[12]

Limited violent conflict consistently occurred throughout Somali history. Pastoral groups fought over water rights and other resources. While Somalis valued warriors, they did not establish standing armies. Instead they fought battles using guerrilla techniques with ad hoc units and shifting alliances. Sub-clans may fight against each other one day, then regroup to fight together against a common enemy. As the Somali proverb states, "Me and my clan against the world; Me and my family against my clan; Me and my brother against my family; Me against my brother."[13] Allegiance may follow patrinally (*tol*) or from the mother's brother' side (*rer abti*) or through marriage (*hidid*),[14] allowing for multiple avenues for creation or destruction of alliances.

Diya-paying groups or blood compensation groups form the smallest, most stable organizational unit. These groups consist of a few hundred male heads of related families who contract to receive compensation for injuries of death within the group and provide common defense and assistance.[15] *Diya*-paying groups along with clan elders, traditional law and religious leaders would historically limit clan violence, but as their authority diminished, violence including against non-combatants increased.[16] Colonial rule from the late 1800s decreased the authority of traditional leaders and after independence various governing regimes reduced or manipulated traditional leaders for their own ends. Given Somalia's tribal structure and its peoples proud independence, Somalia's first and each successive government has had difficulty building a strong central government.

Somalia's first independent government headed by a president, prime minister and cabinet consisted of representatives from major parties in northern and southern Somalia and from the major clan groups.[17] Differences soon emerged in the young democracy as it faced discontent from northern Somalis in the former British Protectorate. In 1961 they voted against the provisional constitution, although Southern Somalis voted overwhelmingly in favor of it, thus forecasting Somaliland's future claim of independence.[18] A more pressing problem arose in Somalia's attempt to unite with Somalis living in Northern Kenya. Somalia broke relations with Britain after its decision to not allow Northern Kenya to join Somalia before Kenya's independence in 1963.[19] The decision led to four years of guerilla fighting in Northern Kenya before Somalia's new Prime Minister Mohamed Egal, in 1967 decided to improve relations with Kenya and Ethiopia against whom Somalia had briefly fought over the Ogaden region. Egal also declared that Djibouti belonged to France.

Egal's decision to scale back the unification goal negatively affected the stability of his government. Somalis lost confidence in the government after its foreign policy failures and accused Egal of capitulating by negotiating with Somalia's neighbors. Somalis also lost confidence because the government failed to develop the economy or provide a transparent accountability for government finances.[20] The goal of a Greater

Somalia may have bound Somalis together, but it cost Somalia in terms of development. Instead of using funds obtained during its early independence, Somalia used these funds for its army and to support refugees resulting from conflicts with Ethiopia, Kenya and Djibouti.

Dependant on foreign aid, the country began to divide along clan lines as groups competed for control of that aid. Politics mirrored the competition for resources and in Somalia's last democratic election 1,002 candidates from 62 different parties competed for 123 seats in the National Assembly.[21] In October 1969 when a bodyguard killed Somalia's president, Abdirashid Sharmarke, the military took over the government with no opposition.

Major General Said Barre led the "bloodless revolution." Upon taking power, the military suspended the "constitution, overthrew the perceived leading politicians and banned all parties."[22] The new government's ideology was "Scientific Socialism," a system that combined state control of the economy, nationalism, rejection of clan identity and rural education.[23] The regime went so far as to burn and bury effigies representing tribalism.[24] In 1977 Barre's government reached the height of its popularity after the success of its campaign in the Ogaden. In 1978 it soon fell in esteem, after Ethiopians with Soviet help, defeated Barre's army.[25] The defeat became a turning point in Barre's hold on Somalia.

That same year military members attempted a coup that led to guerilla fighting in central Somalia. Then in 1981, the Somali National Movement (SNM), an Isaaq-dominated insurgent group in the former British Protectorate, established itself to defeat Barre's government.[26] Conflict between Barre and the SNM continued during the 1980s, leading to a violent clash between government and SNM fighters. This fighting resulted in the deaths of approximately 50,000 Isaaq and the displacement of 650,000 people into Ethiopia and Djibouti,[27] after Barre's forces turned its weapons on civilians having failed to defeat the SNM.[28] Under these pressures Barre became even more autocratic and centralized power in Darod subclans associated with his family. During the 1980s Barre lost so much control that Somalis referred to him as "the mayor of Mogadishu."[29]

During the 1980s the Somali economy began to falter. The Barre regime mismanaged it with experiments in state farming and rangeland nationalization. The pastoralist method of raising livestock had been Somalia's chief livelihood, however, Barre's policies restricted pastoralists to ranches that limited their access to scarce resources and damaged the environment.[30] In addition, as the Barre government took in less income, it rewarded connected officials with farmland near the Shabelle and Juba rivers, expelling farmers who had worked the land for generations.[31]

Even from the colonial period, Somalia required foreign aid to supplement its national budget. At independence some argued that Somalia did not have a sufficient infrastructure; without railroads, highways, an airport or even large enough port; to support a sovereign nation. Moreover, the country required massive amounts of foreign aid to function.[32] In the 1950s and 1960s Somalia received hundreds of millions of dollars of aid,[33] yet even this amount of aid did not suffice to uplift the Somali standard of living. In 1969 residents of Mogadishu still bought their water from street peddlers.[34]

Somalia consistently received foreign aid, but the last years of the Barre government saw it rise to unprecedented levels of the country's economy. During the Barre government's last decade, approximately 75 percent of Somalia's resources came from foreign aid.[35] This aid gave Barre another means to hold onto power. Those clans closest to him received patronage, but those clans he disfavored had to fend for themselves. With no other institutions to seek support from, Somalis turned to their clan.[36] However, by the late 1980s with the end of the Cold War foreign aid dried up. Barre's ruthless attack against the SNM and Isaaq people in Northern Somalia, now the self-declared independent nation of Somaliland, turned away Western donors including the U.S. who had donated $680 million.[37]

Barre's system of patronage and pitting clan against clan set the stage for the warlords that dominated the 1990s and early 2000s. After military build-ups financed by Cold War patronage, the clans had access to modern weapons, but exhibited less traditional restraint on the use of violence. As Ioan Lewis wrote, "Hence the political geography of the Somali hinterland in 1992 closely resembled that reported by European explorers in the nineteenth century, with spears replaced by Kalashnikovs and bazookas."[38]

The regime fell in 1991 and Somalia has not had a functioning central government since then. The UN held peace conferences in 1993 in Addis Ababa and in Kenya in 1994. During the 1990s 11 different international conferences met in order to reconcile powerful warlords and form a government. They all failed when each warlord believed that he should be the president of the country.[39] Frustration with the national peace processes guided leaders in northeast Somalia to form their own regional government of the Puntland State of Somalia in August 1998 as a non-secessionist state. The majority of Puntlanders are from the Mijerteyn Darod clan. Puntland and Somaliland fight for control over regions between their provinces.[40]

During the late 1990s various peace conferences focused on local efforts, such as those in Somaliland, not national agendas. However the Arta Conference in 2000, sponsored by the President of Djibouti reestablished the focus on the central government. While ultimately failing to produce a lasting peace, the Arta Conference established the Transitional National Government (TNG) based on the 4.5 clan distribution of offices still in practice today. The 4.5 formula allotted representation based on clan identification. The four major clans received equal numbers of offices and the minor clans half. Initially, the Arta conference diminished the power of the warlords and resulted in a government that had the support of most Somalis and the international community. However, Ethiopia did not support the TNG, a powerful warlord set to become the future president of Somalia did not support the TNG and eventually Islamists in the TNG clashed with more pro-business leaders. The TNG fell apart in 2002.

In 2004 the Transitional Federal Government (TFG), replaced the TNG and is the current ruling administration in Somalia. While the Hawiye dominated the TNG, the Darod clan dominated the early TFG. Somalis considered the first TFG president, Abdullahi Yusuf Ahmed, to be in the pocket of Ethiopia.[41] President Yusuf immediately called for African Union troops for support in Mogadishu.[42] Later in 2007 he approved Ethiopian troops to invade Somalia after the Islamic Courts Union (ICU) defeated the TFG and it fled Mogadishu.

The closest to peace Somalia has seen since 1991 occurred during six months of Islamic rule. In 2006 the Islamic Courts Union (ICU) defeated pro-government forces and became the first political entity since the Barre regime's collapse to exert control over most of South-Central Somalia. The ICU's success also concerned Mogadishu warlords who saw their power diminishing with the ICU in control. The warlords then declared the ICU terrorists to gain support from the U.S.[43] Six months after the ICU gained power, Ethiopia invaded Somalia believing itself threatened and provoked by the ICU. Members of the TFG, including President Yusaf welcomed Ethiopian troops much to the derision of most Somalis. "That was about the stupidest thing the president could do, inviting our archenemy onto our soil," said Ahmed Mohammed Suleiman, a member of the Somali Parliament.[44] Ethiopian forces and Somali government forces restored the TFG to power approximately six months later. Ethiopian troops remained in Somalia until a peace agreement was reached in 2009. After the Ethiopians left, Al-Shabaab rapidly took control of southern Somalia. As part of the 2009 peace agreement Yusuf resigned as president. A new TFG was created and Sheik Sharif Sheik Ahmed, a moderate Muslim and former Chair of the ICU became president. His term ends in August 2012.

<u>Results after 20 Years of Civil War</u>

Twenty years of chaos has taken its toll on Somalia. Somalia's gross domestic product is approximately $2.01 billion in 2009 was a decrease from $2.3 in 2005. Its GDP per capita was $220.3 in 2009 was a decrease from $277.2 in 2005. Life expectancy is 53 years for women and 50 years for men. Women bear 6.2 children on average and the child mortality rate is 10 percent, making Somalia the fifth nation in the world for infant mortality. Forested areas make up only 11 percent of Somalia's land.[45] Yet Somalia economy has performed better than would be expected from a collapsed state. Livestock, animal hides, fish, charcoal and bananas are Somalia's principal exports. Livestock accounts for about 40 perdent of GDP and more than 50 percent of export earnings. Somalia's annual growth rate is a healthy 2.6 percent.[46]

Somalia has been blessed with natural resources, a strategic location on the Gulf of Aden and the Indian Ocean, the longest coastline in Africa, a creative business class and available work force. By no means should its people live in fear of the next famine, armed bandit or predatory leader. The Somali Republic began as a state seeking the rest of its nation. Now, separatist regions and self-serving warlords may pull apart what remains of the Republic. Many Somalis approve of separation and others want to maintain the current borders.

Since the irredentist goal of a Greater Somalia has failed, what could bring Somalis together and bind them to a shared identity? What could bind Somalis together beyond clan loyalty? The current central government that might inspire an all-encompassing ideology, instead acts as the greatest impediment to its development.

---

[1]Said S. Samatar, "The Politics of Poetry," *Africa Report* 38, no. 5 (September/October 1993): 16.

[2] Ioan Lewis, *Understanding Somalia and Somaliland* (New York: Columbia University Press, 2008), 109.

[3]Afyare Abid Elmi, *Understanding the Somalia Conflagration: Identity, Political Islam and Peacebuilding* (New York: Pluto Press, 2010), 32-34.

[4]Ibid., 32.

[5]Eliza Griswold, "Hawa Abdi, Doctor; Human-Rights Activist," *The Atlantic* (November 2011), http://www.theatlantic.com/magazine/archive/2011/11/hawa-abdi/ 8664 (accessed 10 December 2011).

[6]Lewis, 5.

[7] Ibid., 6.

[8]Ali Abdi Hersi, "Continuing Governance Crisis in Somalia: The Bitter Fruit of the Somali's Faulty Approach to the Practice of Statehood," *Weer News,* 26 June 2006, http://www.wardheernews.com/Articles_06/june_06/26_Somalia_ Governance.Crisis_Dr.A.Hirsi2.html (accessed 14 January 2012).

[9]Lewis, 3.

[10]Richard H. Shultz, Jr. and Andrea J. Dew, *Insurgents, Terrorists and Militias: The Warriors of Contemporary Combat* (New York: Columbia University Press 2006), 58.

[11]Lewis, 25, 28.

[12]David D. Laitin and Said S. Samatar, *Somalia: Nation in Search of State* (Boulder, CO: Westview Press, 1987), 43.

[13]Shutlz and Dew, 59-63.

[14]Lewis, 50.

[15]Ibid., 28.

[16]Shultz, 96.

[17]Lewis, 34.

[18]Mark Bradbury, *Becoming Somaliland* (London: Progressio, 2008), 34.

[19]AAP-Reuter, "Somalia to Break U.K. Relations," *The Sydney Morning Herald*, 12 March 1963.

[20]Abdisalam Issa-Salwe, *The Collapse of the Somali State: The Impact of the Colonial Legacy* (London: Haan Publishing, 1996), 78.

[21]Bradbury, 35.

[22]Ibid., 36.

[23]Lewis, 40.

[24]Issa-Salwe, 79.

[25]Lewis, 44-45.

[26]Bradbury, 39.

[27]Mark Bradbury and Sally Healy, "Endless War: A Brief History of the Somali Conflict," *Accord 21: Whose Peace Is It Anyway? Connecting Somali and International Peacemaking* (2010): 10.

[28]Issa-Salwe, 99.

[29]Jeffrey Gettleman, "The Most Dangerous Place in the World," *Foreign Policy,* 16 February 2009, http://www.foreignpolicy.com/articles/2009/02/16/the _most_dangerous_place_in_the_world? (accessed 10 January 2012).

[30]Bradbury, 40.

[31]Ahmed I. Samatar, "The Porcupine Dilemma: Governance and Transition in Somalia," *Bildhaan: An International Journal of Somali Studies* 7, no. 6 (2007): 58.

[32]Jay Walz, "Somalia Facing Grave Problems," *New York Times*, 5 July 1960. See also, Editorial, "Now What for Somalia?" *Milwaukee Journal*, 6 July 1960.

[33]See "Somalia–A Dry Hungry Land Manages to Survive," *New York Times*, 31 January 1966. From 1960 to 1965 Somalia received $200,000 in foreign aid.

[34]R. W. Apple, "Somalia: Turmoil in a Land of Proud and Hostile Clans," *New York Times*, 26 October 1969.

[35]Bradbury, 42.

[36]Ibid., 45.

[37]Samatar, 59.

[38]Lewis, 77.

[39]Samatar, 66.

[40]Bradbury and Healy, 12.

[41]Ibid.

[42]Ibid., 13.

[43]Janis Grobbelaar and Jama M. Ghalib, "Security and Reconciliation in Post-Conflict Society: The Matter of Closing the Books in South Africa and Somalia," *Bildhaan: An International Journal of Somali Studies* 7, no. 5 (2007): 9.

[44]Jeffrey Gettleman, "A Killing Strains Somalia's Hold on Its Tenuous Peace," *New York Times*, 29 July 2006.

[45]United Nations, "Somalia Country Profile," United Nations Data, http://data.un.org/CountryProfile.aspx?crName=Somalia (accessed 30 January 2012).

[46]Central Intelligence Agency World Factbook, "Somalia Economy," https://www.cia.gov/library/publications/the-world-factbook/geos/so.html (accessed 30 January 2012).

CHAPTER 3

GOVERNMENT BY THEFT

> Somalis from the diaspora only want to talk about how the international
> community has got things wrong in Somalia. This is my main point: the problem
> doesn't lie with the international community at all. It's us.[1]
> —Abdirazak Fartagg, *TFG Corruption: An Exclusive Report*

> In most of Africa, the state is a contested terrain where different nationalities, sub-
> nationalities, 'ethnic groups' and communities go to fight for the appropriation of
> resources including power. A state which is contested terrain in the sense can only
> be an anarchy of self-seeking and a theatre of war.[2]
> —Claude Ake, *The Feasibility of Democracy in Africa*

Somalis view the transitional governments, which have governed their country as

illegitimate. They did not elect the TFG president or members of Parliament and have

little say in their selection, indeed Somalia held its last civilian election in 1969.[3] In

addition to lacking the legitimacy of elections, the TFG fails to perform. The transitional

governments have rarely controlled more than a few city blocks in Mogadishu. While

Somalia has received copious amounts of foreign aid, the average Somali has seen little

of it. Instead,the TFG's leadership is characterized by corruption, donor-financed peace

conferences in expensive Nairobi hotels, and questionable deals with neighboring

countries to maintain their influence in Somalia.

Lack of decent governance and the failure of Somalis to unite in a common

identity underlie the vast majority of Somalia's problems. Political reform will best

resolve the manifestations of Somalia's failed state, namely famine, inter-clan warfare,

piracy and al-Shabaab's terrorism. Instead of assisting the Somali people, potential rulers

fought over control of Mogadishu and through control of the city, they would control the

rest of the country. However, as far removed and self-serving as the government's

27

behavior has been certain recent developments indicate that meaningful political reform might occur, especially when combined with a resurgence of traditional Somali methods of conflict resolution.

The TFG consists of a president, prime minister, speaker, parliament and various ministers. Clan leaders appoint the members of parliament. The Parliament then elects the President and Speaker. The President appoints the Prime Minister who presides over the executive agencies.[4] The parliament consists of 550 appointed members. The seats are allocated between each of the four major clans (Darod, Digil-Mirifle, Dir, and Hawiye) with a smaller number of seats divided between minority clans. In January 2009 a peace agreement between the TFG and opposition Islamic groups resulted in the addition of 200 seats for Islamic members and 75 seats for various members of civil society.[5] The increase in the number of seats has proved unwieldy. The proposal for the structure of a permanent government in the Garowe II Principles calls for a parliament of 225 members in the Lower House and the creation of an Upper House with 54 members.[6] Writing a constitution has finally become a priority. During its eight years of existence, the TFG has not drafted a new constitution, held elections or properly accounted for the millions of dollars it received in foreign aid or tariffs.

In February 2012 Abdirazak Fartaag, a former Somali finance officer and head of Public Finance Management Unit from 2009 to 2011 published a devastating account of corruption and theft by the Somali transitional government. In the report, Fartaag alleged the TFG did not follow its own budget or basic accounting methods. Specifically, the report states the TFG financed government business by withdrawing large amounts of cash from the Somali Central Bank, but cannot account for where the cash is actually spent, even for cash withdrawals of $800,000. Fartaag describes the executive agencies charged with providing services to Somali as being led by "briefcase ministers." Fartaag said, "They exist to collect their per diems and then go stay in the best hotels in Nairobi. Then tell to the international galleries, saying 'We can't do anything because the international community isn't doing its job.'"[7] While the TFG has criticized Fartaag for making unfounded allegations, other individuals and agencies have documented the TFG corruption as well.

In testimony before the U.S. Congress, a Somali expert discussed an earlier report authored by Fartaag's Public Finance Management Unit that stated during 2009 and 2010 bilateral assistance totaled $75,600,000 but only $2,875,000 could be traced. "The auditors determined that the balance, which represents more than 96 percent of international aid to the TFG, was simply 'stolen' and specifically recommended forensic investigations of the Office of the President, the Office of the Prime Minister, the Ministry of Finance, and the Ministry of Telecommunications, as the most egregious offenders."[8] In 2011 Transparency International, a non-governmental organization that tracks global corruption, ranked Somalia as the most corrupt country in the world based on its survey of international public and private firms on how corrupt they perceive the public sector in various countries. Somalia also ranked as the most corrupt nation from 2007 to 2010.[9]

The United Nations Monitoring Group for Somalia and Eritrea faults Somalia's government for its country's difficulties. In its July 2011 report the Monitoring Group succinctly described the TFG's inability to govern and the effect this has on the country.

The principal impediments to security and stabilization in southern Somalia are the Transitional Federal Government leadership's lack of vision or cohesion, its endemic corruption and its failure to advance the political process. Arguably even more damaging is the Government's active resistance to engagement with or the empowerment of local, de facto political and military forces elsewhere in the country. Instead, attempts by the Government's leadership to monopolize power and resources have aggravated frictions within the transitional federal institutions, obstructed the transitional process and crippled the war against Al-Shabaab, while diverting attention and assistance away from positive developments elsewhere in the country.[10]

The corruption from top officials filters down to the lowest levels of government. As the TFG pays soldiers sporadically and insufficiently, this leads TFG soldiers to rely on bribes or to sell their issued ammunition. In exchange for ammunition the soldiers receive food, medicine or sometimes *khat*, a plant that produces euphoria and excitement when chewed. "The predominant perception in Mogadishu is that the Government and pro-Government forces sell between one third and one half of their ammunition."[11] The Monitoring Group found the corruption so pervasive and encompassing that Somali businessmen prefer rule by al-Shabaab,[12] presumably because of al-Shabaab's predictability and better organization.

"There is no accountability, no rules at all." Fartaag said to *SomaliaReport*.[13] "Civil servants aren't paid 'salaries' they're given 'allowances' which are not paid with any regularity. What happens is that once a civil servant hasn't been paid for a while, he goes to the PM or President- whomever he has personal connections to- who will then write him a letter asking the Central Bank to pay him X amount of dollars."

Instability aids government corruption, since payments for wages or goods must be made in cash as no commercial banks exist in Somalia. Currently, Somalia's financial system consists of the Central Bank of Somalia, remittance companies or *halawa* companies that transmit remittance cash payments from the *diaspora* to local Somalis, and micro-finance institutions in Somaliland and Puntland.[14] The Somali Central Bank holds TFG revenue deposits, but has not effectively protected the Somali Shilling from counterfeit bills and the Bank has not developed regulations to establish commercial banks.[15] Also, until recently, squatters lived in the Central Bank's headquarters.[16]

The effects of Somalia's long-time civil war explain some of the irregularities discussed by Fartaag and the Monitoring Group. The underdeveloped and informal financial system makes accounting difficult. In addition, until recently, the TFG controlled very little actual ground making delivery of social services difficult if not impossible.

Fartaag's report also criticizes the TFG for not collecting available revenue. The TFG did not collect any taxes in 2011, and the TFG collected fewer tariffs and fees at Somalia's ports and airport than had been budgeted. Ironically, al-Shabaab demonstrated effectively how the TFG could increase its revenues. The Monitoring Group estimates that al-Shabaab raises between $70 to $100 million per year from taxation, commerce, contraband, trade, *diaspora* and external assistance. Its taxation system "is far more sophisticated and comprehensive than that of any other Somali authority, including the administrations of Puntland and Somaliland."[17] A prize revenue-maker for al-Shabaab is the Kiamaayo port in southern Somalia where al-Shabaab exhorts import and export taxes. For example, Al-Shabaab fixed a set charcoal export tax of $1.20 per sack leaving the Kismaayo port.[18]

Fartaag's description of the financial workings of the TFG and the Monitoring Group's report observations dovetail with the chapter's opening quote from Claude Ake, a Nigerian political scientist. The Somali government exists in a "theatre of war" and in

31

"all versus all" struggle to claim the country's resources. The Somali government like some other post-colonial African governments continued the same colonial practice of arbitrary, totalistic and state-centric rule.[19] "The premium on power was so high that the appetite for power was insatiable. That frames a competition for power in which workable power-sharing arrangements do not hold because power is too important to respect such arrangements . . . and because there is nothing to guarantee power-sharing arrangements or anything else except power."[20] Ake's prescription for good governance in Africa is democracy based on African culture and decisionmaking through negotiated consensus.[21]

Corruption even of the magnitude of Somalia's did not cause the state to fail. Rather, the government's lack of connection to its people and lack of accountability to its citizens caused it to fail. In Somalia, the state does not exist for the welfare of its citizens or even to fulfill goals of foreign expansion or ideological goals, Instead the state exists for the betterment of a tightly knit ruling class.

For decades, even before the Barre government's fall, the Somali government did not act on behalf of the Somali people, but rather existed to extract as much foreign aid and national treasure as possible for themselves and select clan members. Ironically, the aid meant to assist Somalia instead became a motivation to fight for control of the country. Djbuoti President Ismail Omer Gaileh who hosted the Arta Conference in 2000, blamed the failure of Somalia officials to lead because of their "preoccupation with grabbing as much money as possible and as quickly, even before any new governance is fully installed."[22] Today foreign aid comprises 70 percent of Somalia's budget.[23]

Developing Civil Society

The Somali central government has failed for decades and there appears to be no individual or entity within the government capable of radically changing this trajectory. However, some glimmer of hope exists that Somalis will lay a foundation for governance based on "negotiated consensus." Traditional methods of conflict resolution, the example set by the stability of certain regional governments, and the vitality and independence of the business sector may lead to legitimate counterweights to the central government.

Xeer

Much has been made of Somalis' loyalty to clan and their nomadic lifestyle that eschews submission to any government, much less one located hundreds of miles away. However, a nomadic pastoral economy based on herding camels, sheep and goats over long distances did not mean governance and judicial systems did not exist.[24] Customary tribal law, *xeer,* governs relations between clans and between same clan members. Using precedents in *xeer*, elders judge disputes to maintain peace within the community rather than assign blame for a wrongdoing.[25] While the principle of kinship or clan compels action, so do contractual relationships formed under *xeer*.[26] In other words, tribal loyalty did not solely drive traditional Somali culture. Negotiated agreements between clans and within clans formed part of Somali culture as well and could form the basis of future reconciliation. Indeed, elder-run traditional meetings led to peace in the northern provinces.

Regional Governments

Parts of Somalia have experienced stability since the 1990s. The northern provinces of Somaliland and Puntland have had stable and democratically elected governments for many years. Located closer to central Somalia, the Gaalmudug, and Himan and Heeb regional governments provide peace and stability as well. Taken together, these regions compromise over half of Somalia.[27] These regional governments developed on their own initiative based on local reconciliation and negotiation.[28] Somaliland is the longest running and most successful of these regional governments.

The self-declared independent country of Somaliland contrasts sharply with southern Somalia. The former British Protectorate has maintained a stable, democratic government almost since inception. Many have examined the reasons behind Somaliland's stability compared to southern Somalia. Somaliland's lack of natural resources and lack of foreign aid meant that no grand prize existed to instigate disputes. Shared suffering under Said Barre's targeted repression of the northern state led to the creation of a political movement to fight the regime and created a shared identity among Somalilianders. During the colonial era, the British governed less intrusively than the Italians, leaving more traditional organization in place. Also, fewer clans live in Somaliland with the Isaaq clan holding the majority.

In addition to not having riches that inspired conquest, Somaliland's lack of resources meant that the government needed financial and political support from its people in order to survive. The government could not legislate from above without consent from below. "Revenue bargaining" meant that for the Somaliland government to fund its military and other state goals, it had to give rights and representation to its citizens to receive their financial backing.[29]

In 1992 Somaliland declared its independence from Somalia. The SNM, the political party that led the fight against the attacking forces of the Barre regime, initially led the new government. While the Isaaq clan dominated the SNM, sub-clans within the Isaaq did not agree with SNM predominance in the government. For example, the Ilse Muse sub-clan controlled the Berbera port, but was not well-represented with the SNM. Ilse Muse resisted attempts by the SNM to take control of the port in order to receive taxation revenue to fund the Somaliland Army.[30] Unable to defeat the Ilse Muse, the SNM agreed to negotiate. Three peace conferences followed the agreement to negotiate. The negotiations resulted in widening the participation in the Somaliland government of differing sub-clans and resulted in a new National Charter that divided the government into a presidential executive, independent judiciary and bicameral legislature that included an upper house of clan elders.[31]

Lack of international recognition meant that Somaliland received little international financial support. "As a result, the Somaliland government has never received international financial assistance. This is not to say that it does not receive any aid, only that the small amount of aid it receives is directly administered by local NGOs and aid agencies."[32]

Business Acumen

Even without stability or a functioning government, some Somali businesses survived and performed well. *Halawa* companies in Somalia receive over $1 billion a year from the diaspora to the homeland. Somalia's cell phone service is the best in Africa and Somali trading skills are well regarded all over Africa. A Kenyan Somali describes the business sense of Somali immigrants, "We were not traders until these people arrived," he told *The Africa Report*. "They have been successful because of how they do business. Instead of selling two shirts a day at a huge profit, the Somali trader tries to sell 200 at a minimal profit." In Eastleigh, a section of Nairobi inhabited primarily by Somali immigrants, 13 major banks recently opened with hours adjusted for Easleigh's 24 hour, seven day a week economy.[33]

The increased security resulting from the success of AMISOM troops has inspired more business and even exploration of Somalia's energy resources. "Every time they seized territory they (AMISOM) would make a defensive ring. I concluded that the peace in Mogadishu is more durable than it has been in the recent past because the East African troops will be here for the foreseeable future," Liban Egal, a Somali-American businessman told Kenya's, *The Daily Nation*. "The people, too, are tired of war and don't care about clannism. All they want is peace and they don't care who leads."[34] Egal intends to establish the First Somali Bank and other projects such as a fish farm, research livestock production and create a software company to mange the government's payroll.[35] Egal described his own experience with Somali corruption. After he arrived, central bank officials asked for a $100,000 registration fee. "I said, a hundred thousand dollar, for what?" he said and refused to pay. When asked about this a government spokesman in an email wrote, "Hahahahaha, this is absolutely not true . . . Corruption is the thing of the past."[36]

In January 2012 a Canadian Oil Company, Africa Oil Corporation, began drilling the first oil in Somalia in 20 years. Africa Oil believes that the Dharoor Block in Puntland may contain one billion barrels of oil.[37] Notwithstanding the threat that large deposits of natural resources like oil may lead to autocratic government, the growing business sector means more Somalis and more groups of Somalis acting together will have the financial ability to negotiate for representation and accountability.

Businessmen from different clans worked together for the sake of their business over clan loyalty. A Somali businessman said, "merchants from different clans own shares of most big companies in Somalia. If they can share business (profit and loss) Somalis can also share power too."[38] Businesses operate across regions and across clans, which promotes peace. "In Mogadishu, many telephone repairmen, petty traders, drivers and company or business guards are former gunmen. Business also finances clan elders in peacemaking processes and usually pays the costs of inter-clan meeting venues, transport and lunches."[39]

Whether or not the development of these components of civil society will alter the practices of the Somali government, its form will soon change. Frustrated by the corruption, the international community at the London Conference on Somalia in February 2012 called for the creation of the Joint Financial Management Board that will include both Somali and international representatives to ensure foreign aid and domestic resources serve the public interest.[40] Fed up with eight years of intransigence, the international community has emphatically stated that aid to the TFG will end in August 2012 and that no further extensions would be granted.[41] Numerous current Somali politicians are already positioning themselves for the transition by forming new political parties and declaring their intention to run for President. However, a unifying leader or party has yet to emerge.

Absent a drastic change for good or ill, Somalia should continue its slow march towards finding national unity and stability. Somalis do not want the continued intransigence, but national leaders have no incentive to move the process faster. Indeed, writing in January 2012 after the rout against al-Shabaab had begun, U.S. intelligence agencies see little evidence that a turnaround will occur soon. "The TFG and its successor almost certainly will be bogged down with political infighting and corruption that impede efforts to improve security, provide basic services, or gain popular legitimacy. The TFG is certain to face persistent attacks from al-Shabaab."[42]

---

[1]Abdirazak Fartagg, "Audit Investigative Report–2011: Transitional Federal Government, Somalia," *Somalia Report,* 20 February 2012, http://somaliareport.com/downloads/Audit_Investigative_Report___2011_Consolidatedx.pdf (accessed 27 March 2012).

[2]Claude Ake, *The Feasibility of Democracy in Africa* (Dakar, Sengal: Council for the Development of Social Science Research in Africa, 2000), 167.

[3]Ioan Lewis, *Understanding Somalia and Somaliland* (New York: Columbia University Press, 2008), 37.

[4]Somali Republic, "Somali Transitional Charter, Transitional Federal Charter for the Somali Republic," http://www.unhcr.org/refworld/country,,,LEGISLATION, SOM,456d621e2,4795c2d22,0.html (accessed 28 March 2012).

[5]US Department of State, "Background Note:Somalia," http://www.state.gov/r/pa/ei/bgn/2863.htm#gov. (accessed 29 March 2012).

[6]Somali National Conference, "Communique from Garowe Second Somali National Consultative Constitutional Conference," 17 February 2012, Raxanreeb.com, http://www.raxanreeb.com/2012/02/somalia-communique-from-garowe-second-somali-national-consultative-constitutional-conference/ (accessed 30 March 2012), 5.

[7]Jay Bahadur, "TFG Corruption: An Exclusive Report. Part II: Of Budgets and Briefcase Ministries," *Somalia Report,* 27 February 2012, http://somaliareport.com/index.php/post/2938/TFG_Corruption_An_Exclusive_Report/// (accessed 29 March 2012).

[8]US House of Representatives Committee on Foreign Affairs, *Prepared Remarks of Dr. J. Peter Pham, Director, Michael S. Ansari Africa Center Atlantic Council,* Subcommittee on Africa, Global Health, and Human Rights and Subcommittee on Terrorism, Nonproliferation, and Trade, 7 July 2011. See also, John Norris and Bronwyn Bruton, *Twenty Years of Collapse and Counting: The Cost of Failure in Somalia* (Washington, DC: Center for American Progress and One Earth Future Foundation, September 2011).

[9]Transparency International, "Corruption Perceptions Index for 2007-2011," http://www.transparency.org/policy_research/surveys_indices/cpi, (accessed 13 February 2012). The Index measures perceived corruption of 183 countries.

[10]United Nations Monitoring Group, S/2011/433, *Report of the Monitoring Group on Somalia and Eritrea Pursuant to Security Council Resolution 1916* (18 July 2011), 12.

[11]Ibid., 44.

[12]Ibid., 12.

[13]Jay Bahadur, "TFG Corruption: An Exclusive Report. Part I: The Cash Kleptocracy," *Somalia Report*, 21 February 2012, http://www.somaliareport. com/index.php/post/2855/TFG_Corruption_An_Exclusive_Report (accessed 27 March 2012).

[14]African Development Bank-African Development Fund, "Somalia Country Brief," February 2010, http://www.afdb.org/fileadmin/uploads/afdb/Documents/ Project-and-Operations/SOMALIA%20-%20Country%20Brief.pdf. (accessed 28 March 2012).

[15]Bahadur, "TFG Corruption Report Part I."

[16]Murithi Mutiga, "Modgadishu Rumbles Back to Life as the Shabaab Falters," *The Daily Nation,* 3 March 2012.

[17]UN Monitoring Group, 27.

[18]Ibid., 199.

[19]Ake, 36.

[20]Ibid., 38.

[21]Ibid., 123.

[22]Ahmed I. Samatar, "The Porcupine Dilemma: Governance and Transition in Somalia," *Bildhaan: An International Journal of Somali Studies* 7, no. 6 (2007): 69.

[23]Fartaag.

[24]Lewis, 3, 50.

[25]Joakim Gundel, "The Predicament of 'Oday:' The Role of Traditional Structures in Security, Right, Law and Development in Somalia," Danish Refugee Council and Novib/Oxfam, November 2006, http://www.logcluster.org/ops/som/infrastructure-communication-various/Gundel_The%20role%20of%20traditional%20structures.pdf (accessed 30 March 2012), 8.

[26]Jama Mohamed, "Kinship and Contract in Somali Politics," *Africa* 77, no. 2 (2007): 226-249.

[27]UN Monitoring Group Report, 11.

[28]Ibid.

[29]Nicholas Eubank, "Taxation, Political Accountability, and Foreign Aid: Lessons from Somaliland," *Journal of Development Studies* (26 March 2011), http://ssrn.com/abstract=1621374 (accessed 26 March 2012).

[30]Eubank, 10.

[31]Ibid., 11.

[32]Ibid., 6.

[33]Parselelo Kantai, "Inside Garissa Lodgo, Nairobi's Somali Trading Hub," *The Africa Report,* 31 January 2011, http://www.theafricareport.com/index.php/east-horn-africa/inside-garissa-lodge-nairobi-s-somali-trading-hub-5136196.html (accessed 24 March 2012).

[34]Mutiga.

[35]Ibid.

[36]Jeffrey Gettleman, "A Taste of Hope in Somalia's Battered Capital," *The New York Times*, 3 April 2012.

[37]Eduard Gismatullin, "Vancouver-based Africa Oil Defies Al-Qaeda in Billion-Barrel Somali Well Drill," *The Vancouver Sun*, 5 March 2012.

[38]Afyare Abid Elmi, *Understanding the Somalia Conflagration: Identity, Political Islam and Peacebuilding* (New York: Pluto Press, 2010), 41.

[39]Anonymous Somali Writer, "Business as Usual, Bakaaro Market in War," in *Accord 21: Whose Peace Is It Anyway? Connecting Somali and International*

Peacemaking, ed. Mark Bradbury and Sally Healy (London: Consiliation Resources, 2010): 68.

[40]"London Conference on Somalia: Communique, Annex A: Declaration by the Initial Members of the Joint Financial Management Board at the London Conference," 23 Februay 2012, Foreign and Commonwealth Office of the UK, http://www.fco. gov.uk/resources/en/pdf/global-issues/731221182/communique-annexa (accessed 19 March 2012).

[41]London Conference on Somalia: Communique.

[42]James R. Clapper, Director of National Intelligence, *Unclassified Statement for the Record on the Worldwide Threat Assessment of the US Intelligence Community to the Senate Select Committee on Intelligence*, 31 January 2012, 19.

CHAPTER 4

LAND OF NOMADS

It is Goha that life sustains
O' pride of the home
antelope-like she-camel
noblest of animals all surely she
the furry-necked she-camel
with belly huge
sour milk abundant produces she
you, curly-furred camel of mine.[1]
   —the "Mad Mullah," Sayyid Mohammed Abdile Hassan
   Camel Milk a Source of Sustenance for Somalis

The neat distinction between internal security and national security proves to be merely academic in the case of Somalia.[2]
   —Janis Grobbelaar and Jama Ghalib, *Security and Reconciliation*

Beyond causing poor governance, the lack of agreement on what constitutes the nation of Somalia resulted in conflicts with Somalia's neighbors and among Somalia's provincial governments. The lack of a legitimate central government and national unity meant that provincial governments, clan leaders or warlords would seek the assistance of neighboring countries to support their individual agendas often at the expense of other Somalis. If a clan leader wanted more authority, the leader might ask Ethiopia or Kenya to support his agenda rather than negotiate with the federal government. This same negotiation tactic proved successful when dealing with the international community. In Somalia the concepts of recognized, stable borders, governing legitimacy and territorial ownership differ from most modern standards.

Traditional Somali culture revolves around the nomad and the family's herd of grazing camels, goats and sheep. The above poem written by the "Mad Mullah," Sayyid

Mohammed Abdile Hassan leader of a successful anti-colonial movement in the early 1900s, describes Somali veneration for the camel as the animal best suited for Somalia's harsh, arid environment. The environment may require a pastoral herder to travel hundreds of miles to find food and water for his animals.[3] The camel is central to Somali culture as it provides sustenance in an unforgiving environment and the requirements for raising camels form the organization for traditional society. A Somali can survive for six months on camel's milk and urban Somalis still send their children to live with nomadic family members as a way to "toughen them up." With this nomadic orientation, Somali political movements focused on reclaiming Greater Somalia.

Neat politically defined borders meant little compared to every day experience of traversing traditional grazing routes. The Mad Mullah, known as the first Somali nationalist, galvanized Somalis to fight the British and Ethiopians for control over land occupied by ethnic Somalis. Other nationalist movements from the founding democracy, to the dictatorship of Said Barre to Al-Shabaab's goal of uniting all of the Somali people under the Sharia law,[4] focused on the broad concept of Greater Somalia and not on Somalia's internationally recognized borders.

As discussed in chapter 3, the very founding of Somalia entailed projecting power into neighboring countries in order claim lands peopled by ethnic Somalis. National unity came at the cost of another nation's territory. The boundaries set by colonial powers made sense according to European national interest, but not African interests. Throughout the 1900s, even after independence, East Africans regularly crossed international boundaries to make use of traditional grazing routes, undergo pilgrimages to sacred sites or crossed borders to seek refuge from drought and famine.[5] Even with these migrations

43

of people after the colonies gained independence in the 1950s and 1960s, regional

organizations and most national governments believed that the colonial era borders

should remain to avoid instigating conflict across the continent,[6] although these borders

ideally would not have been established since they did not align with the locations of

traditional populations.

Somalia's internationally recognized boundaries do not fit neatly with Somali

history, economy or society. Consequently, the formation of a national government with

ties to regional and local governments is difficult. A more reasonable state organization

would be a larger state that encompasses all ethnic Somalis or smaller regional entities

that preserve traditional grazing rights and where individuals have a connection with

those having authority. A national government that local people have no connection to

and does not inspire ethnic unity, especially one that has proven to be corrupt and

predatory (whether as a democracy, scientific socialist, dictatorship or transitional

government). The problems of establishing a modern state also influenced Somalia's

relations with its neighbors, Ethiopia and Kenya.

Regional Politics

The predominately Christian Ethiopia and the overwhelmingly Muslim Somalia

fought for centuries for the Horn's control. After colonization divided East African

nations, Ethiopia found that it needed its own port for trade and national security. After

World War II Ethiopia asked the Great Powers to add Somaliland with its port at Berbera

and lengthy coastline along the Gulf of Aden to its territory.[7] Since Somalia's

independence in 1960, Somalis and Ethiopians invaded each other's territory on three

separate occasions. Somalia sustained low-level conflict with Ethiopia over the Ogaden region, populated by Somalis, from 1961 to 1967. In 1977 Somalia successfully invaded Ethiopia to claim the Ogaden only to be defeated and driven out a year later.[8]

In 2006 with the Somali Transitional Federal Government's approval, Ethiopia invaded Somalia and stayed until 2009 in order to defeat the Islamic Courts Union which had wrested control of Somalia from the TFG.[9] Ethiopia, the TFG and the U.S. believed the ICUs fundamentalism and possible links to Al-Qaeda warranted toppling the Islamic government. In 2001 the U.S. designated the ICU's religious leader, Hassan Dahir Aweys, as a terrorist.[10] Later, Awyes stated the ICU's desire was to unify the Somali people, "We (the ICU) will leave no stone unturned to integrate our Somali brothers in Kenya and Ethiopia and restore their freedom to live with their ancestors in Somalia."[11]

In July 2006 Aweys told Somalis to prepare for a holy war with Ethiopia, because of the ICU's concerns that Ethiopia would support the TFG. "We must defend our sovereignty," Aweys said. "I am calling on the Somali people to wage a jihad."[12] In December 2006 Ethiopia eventually invaded Somalia, because it believed itself threatened by the ICU and its call for Muslim fighters around the world to join. Ethiopia is an historically Christian country, even though Muslims make up half of Ethiopia's population. "What did you expect us to do?" said Zemedkun Tekle, a spokesman for Ethiopia's information ministry. "Wait for them to attack our cities?"[13] The Ethiopians quickly defeated the ICU forces that held their ground while other supporters vanished from ICU controlled cities. The victory proved short-lived as ICU and fundamental Islamic fighters then waged an underground counterinsurgency war that resulted in a peace deal and the withdrawal of Ethiopian troops in early 2009. Al-Shabaab remained in control of much of southern Somalia until recently and the TFG required troops from the

African Union to support their government. After AMISOM troops succeeded in retaking

Mogadishu from Al-Shabaab, Ethiopian troops routed Al-Shabaab units first in towns

located near the Ethiopian-Somali border then later the towns of Baidoa and El Bur closer

to the center of Somalia. Ethiopia does not intend on occupying Somali cities, and plans

to relinquish control to AMISOM.[14]

Ethiopian hesitancy to stay in Somalia stems from its history of interference in

Somali politics. Ethiopians intervened in Somalia not simply when faced with a direct

threat such as Al-Shabaab, but because of lingering suspicions of Somalia's irredentist

goals and desire for access to the Red Sea. Ethiopia supported such anti-government

groups as the Somali Salvation Democratic Front (SSDF) in Puntland in the 1980s and

the SNM in Somaliland during the 1990s. In the 2000s Ethiopia supported the Somali

Restoration and Reconciliation Council (SRRC) a group of warlords and clan leaders in

southern Somalia, primarily Mogadishu, who opposed the Transitional National

Government.[15] Former director of the Eastern Africa Standby Brigade and now a member

of the Ugandan Parliament, Simon Mulongo describes a web of competing interests

among the states intervening in Somalia for access to resources and control over

provincial governments. "For Ethiopia, it is about control of the sea."[16] Mulongo said.

"The Ogaden war still lingers in the minds of Ethiopians. They cannot just sit back and

allow the formation of a semi-autonomous Jubaland region led by the Kenyans. It will

obviously reopen the Ogaden issue."

Kenya and Eritrea maintained less constant involvement in Somalia than Ethiopia,

but still influence Somali security and politics. Eritrea involvement in Somalia relates to

its adversarial relationship with Ethiopia and the opportunity to weaken it by supporting factions in Somalia opposed to them. Eritrea gained its independence from Ethiopia in

1993 after a 30-year war. From 2005 to the present, Eritrea provided arms to Al-Shabaab

and other opposition groups, a charge Eritrea denies.[17] In 2007, after Ethiopia invaded

Somalia and dispersed the ICU, Eritrea hosted a meeting for Islamists and other

opposition groups that led to the formation of the Alliance for the Re-liberation of

Somalia (ARS).[18] In 2008 the transitional government and certain sections of ARS

reached a peace agreement.

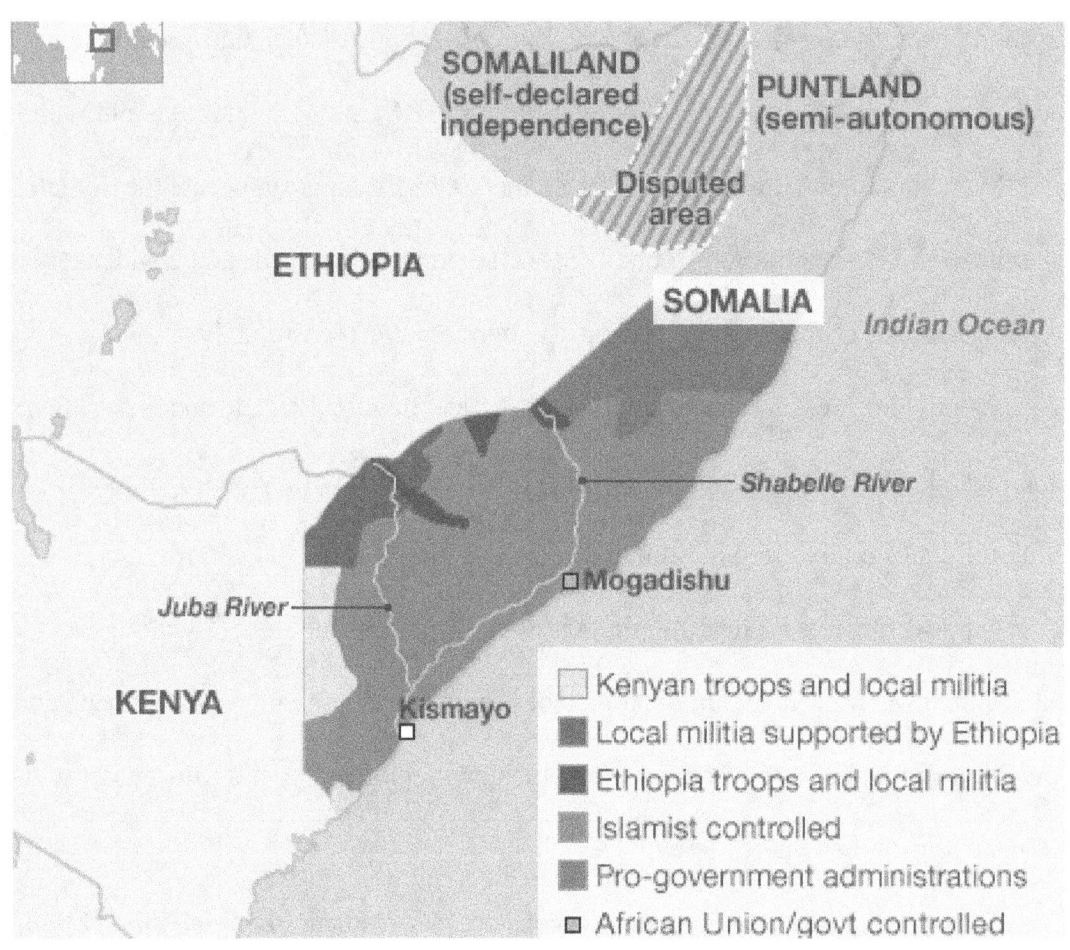

Kenya's interests concern the effect of Somalia's instability on its security. In October 2011 Kenyan troops invaded Somalia, its first foreign military engagement.[19] Several factors prompted the incursion. Before the invasion, actors from Somalia kidnapped several tourists from Kenya's coast and also two aid workers from the Dabaab refugee camp. The kidnappers brought the hostages back to Somalia and held them for ransom. The kidnapping damaged Kenya's robust tourist industry and proved to be the last straw for Kenya's tolerance for its unstable northern neighbor. Since the 1990s, Kenya hosted the Dabaab refugee camp. It is the largest refugee camp in the world and populated mostly by Somalis.[20] In addition to refugees, Somalia exported and continues to export terrorism. Al-Shabaab recruits young Kenyans and its influence spreads in the region. Since October Kenyan troops defeated Al-Shabaab from a number of Somali cities. Kenyan troops will soon be re-hatted as AMISOM troops with funding from the AU.

Finally, of its immediate neighbors, Somalis view Djibouti's involvement favorably for its assistance in attempting to reach peace by hosting reconciliation conferences.[21]

Local Governments

The emergence of local governments presents both the opportunity to build functioning locally-controlled government and also the danger of Balkanization. Somaliland declared its independence from the central government and other provincial governments like Puntland want to remain a part of Somalia, but with autonomy. Division does not stop at the larger regional level, however. Several smaller sub-sets of these regions indicated their desire for separation from provincial governments and formation of their own local government. Another complication concerns the policies of Ethiopia and Kenya in terms of supporting local border governments in Somalia to provide a buffer zone between their countries and Somalia's chaotic center. For example, Ethiopia supports various factions of Ahlu Sunna wal Jama'a (ASWJ), a moderate Sufi group and Kenya supports the "Azania State" in southern Somalia.[22]International support complicates the issue as foreign governments and non-governmental organizations provide support to certain local and regional governments due to the central government's inability.

Three examples demonstrate the potential centrifugal forces of localization. First, in the Sool administrative region, a contested area between Somaliland and Puntland, the Sool Sanaag Cayn Army (SSCA), a clan-based militia, fights against regional authorities in order obtain its own autonomy as a recognized region in Somalia.[23] A U.S. and a Canadian citizen lead the SSCA and obtain financial support from the Somali diaspora. Indigenous tribal leaders believe the SSCA exaggerates legitimate issues for the interest of the SSCA's leadership, such as their involvement in Kaalshaale, a dispute over water reservoirs that led to the deaths of 100 people. Elders from the area told the United Nations Monitoring Group that the SSCA "are entirely dependent on external funding. They get money, cause trouble, and use that to raise more money [...] The fighting at Kaalshaale was really between two clans over land, but the SSCA provided ammunition and fuel."[24]

Second, the "Galmudg State," a democratic state formed by residents living in the central regions of Galguduud and Mudug, faces the problem of fragmentation. Smaller sub-clans, such as the Salebaan, Ayr, Dir, Marehan and Shikaal do not accept the

49

Gamudug government. In response militia members of the sub-clans blocked roads and conducted suicide bombings that forced aid agencies to leave the area.[25] To counter the sub-clans, the Galmudug government ordered the clan to give up their weapons; however, the government may not be able to enforce that order given its inability to suppress pirates and kidnappers in the area.[26]

Third, some alleged local governments sprang from nowhere and exist primarily in cyberspace simply to gain support and resources from the international community. The United Nations Monitoring Group on Somalia lists the following so-called local governments as self-serving creations of the diaspora to include the "Awdal State, Maakhir State, Central State, Banaadirland, Xamar iyo Xamar Daye, Midland Republic and many others."[27]

Arguably, stable local governments could form the building blocks for a functioning national government, but not necessarily so. Greed, self-interest and lack of unity trouble regional governments as well.

U.S. Policy Towards Somalia

After removing its forces from Somalia following the Black Hawk Down incident in October 1993, the U.S. did not engage Somalia until 1996. Even after 1996 and approximately for the next decade, the U.S. limited its engagement to a policy of containing Somalia so that instability did not spread.[28] In 2006 American interest in Somalia increased with the ICU's establishment, and its possible terrorist links resulting in the U.S. focusing its efforts on countering terrorist threats.[29] Since 2008 the U.S. supported the TFG, even though the U.S. understood the its limitations. To assist the TFG, U.S. Assistant Secretary of State for African Affairs, Johnnie Carson said the U.S.

"supported them in their efforts to do more service delivery in those areas in which they control-starting micro-finance programs for women and unemployed youth, creating jobs for young men, restocking clinics and opening some small ones, trying to re-open schools and delivering government services."[30] In 2010 the U.S. announced a dual track strategy for Somalia that entails supporting local governments with development projects to increase their governing ability while at the same time engaging the TFG.[31]

However, the U.S. did not originate the dual track strategy. Various attempts to engage Somali clan leaders, civil society and regional administrations occurred previously. In the 1990s the Life and Peace Institute and the UN developed a "building blocks" strategy to create local and district-level administrations across Somalia. The strategy failed.[32] Similar to today's dual strategy approach, the building blocks approach sought to develop stable regional governments that when aggregated would lead to peace on the national level. The building block approach worked in Puntland, but failed in southern Somalia when members of the Hawiye clan could not agree on reopening the Mogadishu airport and other Hawiye wanted to revive a strong central state.[33] The same arguments against the dual track strategy of today dominated the debate over the building block strategy, namely that a regional-focused approach would encourage "secessionism," and would keep Somalia weak for the plunder by neighboring countries.[34]

U.S. diplomats state that they understand the dual track strategy's potential pitfalls and that the U.S. will only assist legitimate local governments with proven ability to provide services. The U.S. does not support secessionist goals, such as Somaliland's desire for its own state. "When it comes to recognizing new African states, America

51

follows the African Union's lead," said the U.S. Special Representative for Somalia

Ambassador James C. Swan. "And the African Union supports a single Somali state."[35]

---

[1]Sayyid Mohammed Abdile Hassan, (the Mad Mullah), "Camel Milk a Source of Sustenance for Somalis," trans. Ahmed Ali Abokor, *Wardheer News,* 29 August 2009, http://wardheernews.com/Articles_09/Aug/29_camel_milk_faisal.html. (accessed 11 April 2012).

[2]Janis Grobbelaar and Jama M. Ghalib, "Security and Reconciliation in Post-Conflict Society: The Matter of Closing the Books in South Africa and Somalia," *Bildhaan: An International Journal of Somali Studies* 7, no. 5 (2007): 9.

[3]Lee V. Cassanelli, *The Shaping of Somali Society: Reconstructing the History of a Pastoral People, 1600-1900* (Philadelphia, PA: University of Pennsylvania Press, 1982), 24.

[4]Ted Dagne, *Somalia: Current Conditions and Prospects for a Lasting Peace,* 7-5700 (Washington, DC: Congressional Research Service, 8 October 2010).

[5]Cassanelli, 259.

[6]Ali Abid Hersi, "Continuing Governance Crisis in Somalia: The Bitter Fruit of the Somali's Faulty Approach to the Practice of Statehood," *Wardheer News*, 26 June 2006, http://www.wardheernews.com/Articles_06/june_06/26_Somalia_Governance. Crisis_Dr.A.Hirsi2.html (accessed 3 April 2012).

[7]Afyare Abdi Elmi, *Understanding the Somalia Conflagration–Identity, Political Islam and Peacebuilding* (London: Pluto Press, 2010), 91.

[8]Kidane Megisteab, "Critical Factors in the Horn of Africa's Raging Conflicts," (Discussion Paper 67, Nordiska Afrikainstitutet, Uppsala 2011), 11.

[9]Ibid.

[10]Ibid. Also see U.S Department of Treasury Office of Foreign Assets Control, "Terrorism: What You Need to Know about U.S. Sanctions," http://www.treasury. gov/resource-center/sanctions/Programs/Documents/terror.pdf (accessed 2 April 2012).

[11]Mohammed Daoud Ahmed, "Solving the Somali Jigsaw," *Think Africa Press,*7 March 2012, http://thinkafricapress.com/somalia/somali-jigsaw. (accessed 13 April 2012).

[12]Jeffrey Gettlemen, "Somalis Say Ethiopian Presence is Just the Uniforms," *The New York Times,* 22 July 2006.

[13] Jeffrey Gettlemen, "Ethiopia Hits Somali Targets, Declaring War," *The New York Times,* 25 December 2006.

[14] Aaron Maasho, "Ethiopian Troops Set to Leave Somalia by End of April: AU," *Somaliland Sun*, 11 March 2012.

[15] Megisteab, 14.

[16] Parselelo Kantai and Patrick Smith, "The Dangers of Carving Up Somalia," *The Africa Report*, 6 February 2011, http://www.theafricareport.com/index.php/news-analysis/the-dangers-of-carving-up-somalia-50180834.html (accessed 10 March 2012).

[17] United Nations Monitoring Group, S/2007/436, *Report of the Monitoring Group on Somalia Pursuant to Security Council Resolution 1724 (2006),* 27 June 2007, 3; United Nations Monitoring Group, S/2008/769, *Report of the Monitoring Group on Somalia Pursuant to Security Council Resolution 1724 (2008),* 20 November 2008, 25. See also Tom Odula, "Eritrea: We Can't Supply Somali Militants Weapons," *Associated Press*, 11 November 2011.

[18] UN Monitoring Group, *Resolution 1724 (2008),* 17.

[19] International Crisis Group, *The Kenyan Military Intervention in Somalia. Africa Report Number 184* (New York: International Crisis Group, 15 February 2012), i.

[20] Ibid., 3.

[21] Elmi, 98.

[22] United Nations Monitoring Group, S/2011/433, *Report of the Monitoring Group on Somalia and Eritrea Pursuant to Security Council Resolution 1916* (18 July 2011), 52, 250.

[23] Ibid., 32.

[24] Ibid., 133.

[25] Aweys Cadde, "Galmudug Demands Clans Hand Over Weapons," *Somalia Report*, 20 March 2012, http://www.somaliareport.com/index.php/post/3111 (accessed 14 April 2012).

[26] Ibid.

[27] United Nations Monitoring Group, *Resolution 1916,* 130.

[28] Senate Committee on Foreign Relations, Subcommittee on African Affairs, *Testimony of Assistant Secretary Johnnie Carson, Bureau of African Affairs, U.S. Department of State: Hearing on Developing a Coordinated and Sustainable U.S.*

*Strategy Toward Somalia before the Senate Committee on Foreign Relations'
Subcommittee on African Affairs*, 20 May 2009.

[29]Ibid.

[30]"Africa: Resolving Conflicts Remains a Top U.S. Policy Priority, Carson Says,"
All Africa, 12 March 2012, http://allafrica.com/stories/201203131400.html (accessed 26
March 2012).

[31]Ibid.

[32]House Committee on Foreign Affairs, Subcommittee on Africa, Global Health
and Human Rights and the Subcommittee on Terrorism, Nonproliferation and Trade,
*Prepared remarks of Bronwyn Bruton Fellow, One Earth Future Foundation: Hearing on
"Assessing the Consequences of the Failed State of Somalia,"* 7 July 2011.

[33]Bradbury and Healy, 13.

[34]Ibid.

[35]Ambassador James C. Swan, "Speech by the U.S. Special Representative for
Somalia" (Ohio State University, 9 November 2011).

CHAPTER 5

PEACE-LORDS NOT PRESIDENTS

The mouth of my grave is open." [1]

–Rachel Pieh Jones, *New York Times*

Upon pregnancy a woman in Somali says the above proverb to others and asks for a prayer for her and her baby. This realism makes sense when bearing a child in Somalia's harsh, austere environment. But no amount of realism prepared Somalia for the realities of the last 20 years.

Countering piracy, terrorism, cross-border kidnapping and regional conflict are all present reasons for international action in Somalia, but the country's humanitarian crisis presents the most compelling reason. The UN estimates that tens of thousands died in last year's famine and many will be in danger of starvation this year as well. During the height of the 2011 famine, each day 13 out of every 10,000 children under the age of five died. When aggregated this figure meant that every 11 weeks, 10 percent of children under the age of five living in stricken areas died to due to famine-related diseases.[2] In the midst of starvation Al-Shabaab blocked humanitarian aid and the TFG failed to effectively assist in distribution. While the UN declared the famine over in late 2011, many areas still face risk. Already the UN's humanitarian coordinator for Somalia requested $1.5 billion for 2012, because of expected low rainfalls, potential famine and continued violence.[3]

With its arid climate, Somalia historically experienced drought, but rarely famine. Human beings, through theft of aid or threats to humanitarian workers, caused the droughts of the early 1990s and 2011 to become catastrophic. On 28 November 2011 Al-

Shabaab banned 16 aid organizations from delivering emergency food aid in Somalia.[4] It had previously banned other organizations, such as the World Food Program in 2010 and held humanitarian workers hostage.[5]

Al-Shabaab's extreme violence prompted Somalis to support the Ethiopian incursion, if it meant defeating the terrorist group. "Brother, let the Ethiopians come because when the drought engulfed us, the Shabaab prevented all kinds of assistance from reaching us," said Leelo Ahmed, a mother of four children in Beledweyne, a town near the Somali-Ethiopian border.[6]

Starvation ranks as only one among many life-threatening perils for Somalis. The government's collapse and resulting chaos has taken a toll on the Somali people and environment. Somalia ranks at the bottom of the world's nations concerning life expectancy, infant mortality and maternal mortality. The World Health Organization states the life expectancy for Somalis is 51 years old, infant mortality rate of 108 deaths per 1000 births and 180 deaths per 1000 live births up to age five. The median population is 18 years. The percentage of those under age 15 is 45 percent; and the percentage of those over 60 years of age is 4 percent. The fertility rate for women is 6.3 children. The adult literacy rate is 62 percent and youth literacy rate is 71 percent. Children receive an average of 2.4 years of school.[7]

Land degradation and deforestation increases the problem of drought and floods. Somali forest and woodland resources represent only 11 percent of Somalia's land area. The charcoal trade caused much of the deforestation and degradation, "where the acacia forests have been cut down for charcoal, such as between the Juba and Shabelle rivers, often becomes unsuitable for grazing, leading to increased conflict over land and water and the displacement of the local population."[8] The United Nations Security Council recently banned the export of charcoal from Somalia mostly to disallow profits from the trade to go to Al-Shabaab. However, even with the ban, it will take time for forests to produce enough to meet local demands for fuel and building materials.[9]

Since 1991 between 450,000 and 1.5 million Somalis have died due to violence or hunger in the ongoing conflict, and more than 2.3 million Somalis either live as refugees or internally displaced persons.[10] These numbers equal almost a third of Somalia's nine million person population. The UN states that 982,000 Somalis registered as refugees in the region with 523,500 living in Kenya, 211,000 in Yemen, 195,000 in Ethiopia, 16,000 in Djibouti and 32,000 in other countries.[11] Somalis predominately occupy the Dadaab refugee camp in Kenya believed to be the largest such camp in the world. By September 2011 over 140,000 new refugees reached Dadaab, swelling the camp's population to 450,000. Planners of the camp intended its capacity to reach 90,000.[12] Ethiopia opened a sixth camp for Somali refugees in June 2011 and planned to open a seventh camp. Djibouti added a refugee camp as well.[13] The rise in population at Dadaab increased insecurity and tension. Administrators stopped registering new refugees, thus they do not know who inhabits the camp. After Kenyan forces entered Somalia, members of Al-Shabaab increased activity at the camp using it as a base for missions in Kenya. "As a result, kidnappings and assaults have become more common, and ominously, improvised explosive device (IED) attacks have also begun to appear with some regularity along the roads within the complex."[14]

The conflict affects not just the current situation, but the foreseeable future as well with children witnessing the fighting. "Students here are not so much interested in learning, because they can see a lot of people carrying guns," Aden Abdi, a 22-year-old English teacher said. "That's what they have in their hearts. Their intention: That they will fight when they grow older."[15] Al-Shabaab forces young boys to join their militias to be used as soldiers or as shields for older fighters. It often attacked schools in order to kidnap children.[16] The group abducts girls as well, forcing younger girls to serve as cooks and cleaners and older girls into sexual relationships.

Across Somalia famine, displacement and lack of governance left women and girls especially vulnerable. With men dead or gone to fight or to tend what remained of livestock, women with children set off for refugee camps on their own. Other women stayed in their villages but were alone, having lost their husbands or fathers to conflict. Members of Al-Shabaab, government forces, and others taking advantage of tribal dislocation raped and abused many young girls and women.[17]

Al-Shabaab offered women and girls to fighters as a means of reward, since financial compensation decreased as AMISOM made territorial gains and the drought reduced taxation revenue. Sometimes the Shabaab members temporarily wed the girls for a few weeks and sometimes simply raped others. A seventeen year-old girl living in a refugee camp described seeing members of Al-Shabaab bury her best friend in the sand then stoned her for refusing to marry one of them. Later the group ganged raped her.[18] Another woman living in an internally displaced person (IDP) camp stated after returning from looking for food, she found a gunman raping her 11 year-old daughter. She fought the man, then other men came kidnapped, beat and burned her with hot plastic.[19] The UN special advisor on sexual violence reported that men in uniform either from TFG or provincial forces frequently rape women in IDP camps at night while they sleep in their huts.[20]

International Response

For all of the above reasons, Somalia calls out for aggressive international intervention due to the scope of the humanitarian crisis and lack of functioning government. Unfortunately, aggressive overt international assistance will most likely cause more harm than good. In one sense, assisting Somalia represents the responsibility of the world community to help another country fallen on hard times. It means giving food to a starving child or medical care to a victim of violence. However, providing assistance to Somalia never proved that simple and extensive foreign engagement invited backlash. For the current crisis, the international community almost assuredly will not conduct a military intervention similar to the UNISOM II mission in early 1990s with its broad mandate. Nnor will it likely impose a more aggressive diplomatic measure such as imposing a limited international administration over the country, as a few have suggested.

The reluctance for wide-scale intervention stems in part from current fatigue with military operations, but also from the realization that aggressive outside action would provide only the shortest possible relief and has little chance of establishing long-lasting change. The world community has learned much since Black Hawk Down.

In March 1993 the U.S. turned over control of the humanitarian mission it led, named Operation Restore Hope, to the UN. Upon the turnover, the UN Operation in Somalia (UNISOM II) became the UN's first peace enforcement mission.[21] Previously, the Cold War had limited the UN's ability to perform large, armed humanitarian missions. With the fall of the Soviet Union, many in the international community hoped the UN could finally perform more assertive action. The UN did so in Somalia by greatly expanding its missions from the limited US mission of providing security for humanitarian relief to the grander goal of nation building. Under United Nations Security Council Resolution 814, the UN's mission became to repatriate refugees, advance political reconciliation with local and regional leaders, establish the Somali police, prosecute violations of international law, remove mines and assist in disarmament.[22]

For this increased mission, UNISOM II was comprised of 28,000 soldiers many from second tier armies, such as Pakistan, and Malaysia with little training. Whereas, the smaller-focused U.S. led mission contained 37,000 soldiers of which 28,000 were U.S. forces. UNISOM II faced a much larger mission, but its leaders lacked knowledge and sensitivity to the political situation in Somalia. A particularly sensitive issue dealt with disarmament. Given the chaotic environment in Mogadishu, clan leaders and individual Somalis believed they needed to be armed and resisted giving up their weapons. Indeed, disarmament became a time-consuming mission in a country awash in weapons from when the Soviets and Americans used Somalia to fight proxy wars.[23] While the UN's expanded peace enforcement mission may have sounded noble to the international community, to General Mohamed Farah Aideed, a leader of one of the Hawiye sub-clans based in Mogadishu and to other warlords, the UN's focus on nation-building and empowering local traditional leaders would undermine their own authority.[24] They resisted UNISOM's objectives. When UN and American forces made Aideed their "center of gravity,"[25] Somalis rallied around another Somali.

In 1992 the U.S. deployed to Somalia not simply acting on humanitarian concerns, but also for political and foreign policy interests. Ordering Operation Restore

Hope demonstrated, according to National Security Advisor Brent Scowcroft, that the U.S. was not "afraid to intervene abroad; it was just that the circumstances weren't right in Bosnia," and it demonstrated the U.S. would intervene on behalf of Muslim victims.[26] The U.S. has no similar interests in Somalia presently, nor does the world community believe any longer that nation-building can be so easily accomplished as the hope that led the UN to approve UNISOM II's expanded mission.

In the future foreign governments and the international community will not respond similarly with such massive international assistance. War fatigue, budget deficits, fears of mission creep may play some role, but also the recognition that those methods will not work in a setting like Somalia. It is not simply fear of soldiers being dragged through the streets or nations into a quagmire that limit mass atrocity response in Somalia, but the realization that this type of assistance will ultimately prove ineffective. Short-term emergency assistance from the international community, even a short-term military intervention like Operation Restore Hope and locally organized long-term programs stand a better chance of success. Fortunately, both groups adeptly offer assistance when provided a secure environment. Armed local groups like the ASWJ and AMISOM troops, consisting of soldiers from the local region have been more widely accepted than the international force in the 1990s.

Peace-Lords

The international community stands ready to assist with humanitarian aid. International aid groups and bilateral aid groups possess the ability to provide enough aid and assistance to those in need. Even in the restrictive environment provided by Al-Shabaab, some aid groups succeeded in negotiating arrangements to provide aid without extortion and other groups provided cash or voucher assistance through cell phone transfers rather than shipping food from overseas. Aid groups found local vendors able to provide food if paid.[27] The United Nation's Consolidated Appeal Process (CAP) for Somalia requests a record-breaking $1.5 billion in donor funds for 2012. The CAP includes 350 projects meant to implement the strategies goals. In addition, Turkey provided a large amount of assistance to Somalia in 2011 and 2012 and it has been widely accepted. Recently, Turkey has launched a number of humanitarian programs in assisting Somalia. Prime Minister Recep Tayyip Erdogan with his wife and daughter visited Somalia in August 2011 and reopened its embassy in Mogadishu later that year. Turkey has raised $300 million for financial aid, will build hospitals, provide garbage trucks for Mogadishu, conduct renovation projects and conduct agricultural development projects.[28]

Somali led organizations provide long-term solutions to hunger, sexual violence and deforestation. Charities founded or run by different women demonstrate effective local solutions to humanitarian and developmental problems. They and women from the diaspora fill many unmet needs. The head of the Somali Women's Federation returned to Somalia after 21 years in Sweden and sees Somali women as national leaders. "We are the peace-lords, we're working hard," she said. "It's the men who left their work –they're just fighting between themselves. Everyone wants to be a president. I tell them, be a president in your own home."[29] Traditionally women served as peacemakers since a marriage often bound two separate tribes together. "Women have no tribes, they have families," Omar said.

Another member of the diaspora, Fatima Jibrell founded the Horn of Africa Relief and Development Organization, now called Adeso, in 1991. Adeso works with local communities to combat deforestation, provide humanitarian aid and support local economies. Adeso provides cash transfers or cash for work programs not food handouts. Their camel caravans reached tens of thousands of nomads by sending workers to walk with pastoralists to teach health care and basic education. The group focuses on the environment with its tie to drought and starvation. "The fact that these vulnerabilities stem from environmental degradation and climate change is similarly often overlooked," said Degan Ali, the executive director. Adeso advocates the building of rock walls to prevent erosion and moving away from charcoal to alternative fuels. "People everywhere have immense potential," Ali said. "And too often I feel that when talking about the Horn of Africa this gets drowned under narratives of hopelessness and destitution."[30]

One of Somalia's most well-known and respected figures for her work with the hungry and with families as an obstetrician and gynecologist is Doctor Hawa Abdi Dhiblawe. In 1991 she began housing Somalis fleeing conflict and famine on her land located outside of Mogadishu. Currently 90,000 people live there. She faced down warlords and Al-Shabaab to keep her refugee camp. When answering what could be done to strengthen civil society in Somalia, she answered, "We can achieve a lot if we put aside clan loyalties and division. Being too proud of someone who died centuries ago will give you nothing . . . The Somali Youth League had only 13 young men. Some of them had not studied let alone attained a professional career, but they were great people because they knew what unity can achieve."[31]

Women in Somalia celebrated International Women's Day in March 2012. Many in Mogadishu wore bright turquoise and white dresses in the print of the Somali flag. "We are wearing the same dresses to show we are organized," said Hawa, a 22-year-old.

Hawa's comment offers more hope for a solution to the humanitarian crisis than raising millions of dollars for aid. Even small numbers of citizens organizing to improve their own country will accomplish more than thousands of outside aid workers. Internal political reform and growth of civil society will form the national unity needed to address crises. Throughout the 1990s, the international community and regional countries intervened aggressively and repeatedly to offer assistance to Somalia. While much could be criticized about how the interventions were conducted, it is unlikely a perfectly conducted operation would put Somalia on the path to peace. At least in Somalia, reconciliation needs to develop first based on discussion with other Somalis. The world community can provide assistance, especially when addressing TFG's corruption, but should not overshadow local efforts.

---

[1]Rachel Pieh Jones, "A Child of Two Worlds," *The New York Times*, 23 February 2012.

[2]United Nations Security Council, S/2011/549, *Report of the Secretary-General on Somalia*, 30 August 2011, 17.

[3]United Nations Office for the Coordination of Humanitarian Affairs, *Consolidated Appeal Process, Somalia 2012*, December 2011, 2.

[4]United Nations Security Council, *Report of the Secretary General on Somalia*, 9 December 2011, 10.

[5]United Nations Monitoring Group, S/2011/433, *Report of the Monitoring Group on Somalia and Eritrea Pursuant to Security Council Resolution 1916*, 18 July 2011, 57-60.

[6]Jeffrey Gettlemen, "Ethiopian Troops Said to Enter Somalia, Opening New Front Against Militants," *The New York Times*, 21 November 2011.

[7]United Nations Educational, Scientific and Cultural Organization (UNESCO), "Statics in Brief, Education Profile Somalia 2009," UNESCO Institute for Statistics, http://stats.uis.unesco.org/unesco/TableViewer/document.aspx?ReportId=121&IF_Langu age=en&BR_Country=7060 (accessed 16 April 2012).

[8]United Nations Security Council, *Report of the Secretary-General on Somalia*, 30 August 2011, 5-6.

[9]United Nations, Food and Agricultural Organization, "Global Forest Resources Assessment 2010, Country Report–Somalia," http://www.fao.org/docrep/013/ al629E/al629e.pdf (accessed 16 April 2012), 5.

[10]John Norris and Bronwyn Burton, "The Price of Somalia's Failure, How Much Has the Collapse of Somalia Cost the World?" *Foreign Policy*, 5 October 2011, http://www.foreignpolicy.com/articles/2011/10/05/the price of failure? (accessed 15 December 2011).

[11]United Nations High Commission for Refugees, "Refugees in the Horn of Africa: Somali Displacement Crisis," http://data.unhcr.org/horn-of-africa/regional.php (accessed 11 May 2012).

[12]United Nations High Commission for Refugees, "UNCHR Country Operations Profile–Kenya," http://www.unhcr.org/pages/49e483a16.html (accessed 11 May 2012).

[13]Deputy Assistant Secretary Reuben Brigety II, Bureau of Population, Refugees, and Migration U.S. Department of State, *Hearing: Assessing the Consequences of the Failed State of Somalia before the House Committee on Foreign Affairs Subcommittee on Africa, Global Health, and Human Rights Subcommittee on Terrorism, Nonproliferation, and Trade*, 7 July 2011.

[14]Center for Strategic and International Studies, "The Dadaab Refugee Complex: A Powder Keg and It's Giving Off Sparks," http://csis.org/print/35548. (accessed 19 April 2012).

[15]Tom Odula, "Somalia's Children Schooled in Guns," *Washington Times,* 14 March 2012.

[16]See United Nations Security Council, S/2011/759, *Report of the Secretary General on Somalia*, 9 December 2011, 14.

[17]UN Office for the Coordination of Humanitarian Affairs, 93.

[18]Jeffrey Gettleman, "For Somali Women, Pain of Being a Spoil of War," *The New York Times,* 27 December 2011.

[19]Lisa Shannon, "The Rape of Somalia's Women Is Being Ignored," *The Guardian,* 11 October 2011.

[20]United Nations, A/66/657-S/2012/33, *Report of the Secretary-General. Conflict-Related Sexual Violence*, 13 January 2012, 13.

[21]Richard J. Norton, "Somalia II," http://www.au.af.mil/au/awc/awcgate/navy/pmi/somalia2.pdf (accessed 2 March 2012).

[22]United Nations, *United Nations Security Council Resolution 814*, 26 March 1993.

[23]Walter S. Poole, *The Effort to Save Somalia: August 1992-March 1994* (Washington, DC: Government Printing Office), 40.

[24]Robert Baumann, Lawrence Yates, and Versalle Washington, *My Clan Against the World: US and Coalition Forces in Somalia 1992-1994* (Ft. Leavenworth, KS: Combat Studies Institute Press, 2004), 79.

[25]Mark Bowden, *Black Hawk Down: A Story of Modern War* (New York: Penguin Books, 1999), 44.

[26]Samantha Power, *A Problem from Hell: America and the Age of Genocide* (New York: Basis Books, 2002), 293.

[27]Tina Rosenburg, "In Famine, Vouchers Can Be Tickets to Survival," *The New York Times*, 27 October 2011.

[28]Recep Tayyip Erdogan, "The Tears of Somalia," *Foreign Policy*, 10 October 2011, http://www.foreignpolicy.com/articles/2011/10/10/the_tears_of_somalia?showcomments=yes (accessed 7 December 2011).

[29]Integrated Regional Information Networks: Humanitarian News and Analysis, "Somalia: Burkas to Tracksuits," 17 April 2012, http://www.irinnews.org/report/95308/SOMALIA-Burkas-to-tracksuits (accessed 19 April 2012).

[30]Hornlighter, "Interview with Degan Ali, Executive Director of Horn Relief," 2 February 2012, http://hornlight.org/2012/02/interview-with-degan-ali-executive-director-of-horn-relief/ (accessed 19 April 2012).

[31]Mire, Sucaad, "Somalia's Nobel Peace Prize Nominee," *Somalia Report*, 24 March 2012, http://www.somaliareport.com/index.php/post/3140/Somalias_Nobel_Peace_Prize_Nominee (accessed 19 April 2012).

CHAPTER 6

A CELL PHONE AND MODERN HIGHWAYS

Poor countries are poor because those who have power make choices that create poverty. They get it wrong not by mistake or ignorance but on purpose.[1]
—Daron Acemoglu and Jams Robinson, *Why Nations Fail*

The most critical (failure of past reconciliation conferences) was the failure to insist on the parties making peace before trying to make a government.[2]
—Ione Lewis, *Understanding Somalia and Somaliland*

A certain irony exists concerning Somalia. In 1993 upon the U.S. relinquishing control of its humanitarian mission in Somalia, the United Nations Operation in Somalia (UNISOM II) became the UN's first peace enforcement mission.[3] After the Cold War ended, the international community held great hope that the UN could finally apply more assertive action to bring peace and development to all nations ravaged by war. Yet 22 years later, the UN's first test case has no functioning government, its people still starve and for the foreseeable future will continue to live in poverty and strife. Why did the international community fail after so much time and attention? Are the Somalis destined to live in chaos with their warring factions armed with modern weapons? Does Somalia represent the failure of international intervention focused on the creation of a stable New World Order or does the failure rest with the Somalis themselves? Does Somalia have anything to teach rest of the world when confronting a failed state?

The practice and policies for international intervention in countries committing atrocities against their own people have developed significantly since 1993. Yet we are far from developing a response that addresses how to assist countries going through a mass atrocity where little or no sense of statehood exists. The international community learned to be adept at providing assistance where a notion of statehood already existed such as in East Timor or Libya. But how do we assist where the global community wants stability more than those with power inside the afflicted country?

The human toll, the wasted aid dollars, the piracy and terrorist threats along with the futility of the last 20 years all cry out for an internationally imposed solution or better, a homegrown solution in Somalia. Indeed, proposed solutions can easily be found. Every Somali news web site and almost every book written about Somalia in recent years contains a plan on how to turn the country around. As one professor joked, a graduate course could be taught "simply by assigning the discourse on the state developed by Somalis through their websites."[4] Ideas and interest in establishing a stable Somalia abound. Lack of well-researched, well-considered proposals does not keep Somalia mired in dysfunction. Rather, since the early 1990s Somalis and the international community have not been able to form a political solution that builds reconciliation.

One State Department official who requested confidentiality described the influence of Black Hawk Down on U.S. foreign policy in the 1990s;

> It was a watershed. The idea used to be that terrible countries were terrible because good, decent, innocent people were being oppressed by evil, thuggish leaders. Somalia changed all that. Here you have a country where just about everybody is caught up in hatred and fighting . . . People in these countries- Bosnia is a more recent example– on't want peace. They want victory. They want power . . . Somalia was the experience that taught us that people in these places bear much of the responsibility for things being the way they are.[5]

Yes, Somalis do bear much of the responsibility for things being the way they are. However, desire for victory developed from Somalia's immediate history where the long-serving dictator, Said Barre, manipulated clan loyalties to maintain power. In addition, Somalia's history since independence to today demonstrates that submitting to the

68

"peace" of a central government without reconciliation between different clans has the real potential of leading to that clan's destruction, such as Barre's persecution of the Isaaq in the late 1980s. Control of the central government means control of foreign aid and other national resources like the port of Mogadishu. Losing control means potentially falling victim to a Barre-like murderous regime.

Creating Unity and Reconciliation

Peace in Somalia requires trust and compromise not simply financial aid and development. Democracy and inclusive government cannot be easily bought. Analysis of Afghanistan's problems with its tribal structure and lack of central government resembles an analysis of Somalia. Fareed Zakaria questioned nation building efforts, stating,"The United States tends to enter wars in developing countries with a simple idea—modernize the country, and you will solve the national security problem [New Gingrich succiently described this theory] We are failing in Afghanistan," Newt Gingrich argued, "because 'we have not flooded the country with highways, we haven't guaranteed that every Afghan has a cell phone, we haven't undertaken the logical steps towards fundamentally modernizing their society . . . '" However, Mr. Gingrich's development argument fails, because it would not remedy the fundamental tribal differences and power-sharing arrangements between Pashtuns, Tajiks and Hazaras.[6]

This analysis holds true for Somalia. Somalis have the best cell phone service in Africa, a keen interest in the outside world. They regularly export their products across the region. The areas where it benefits elites to modernize are modern; but a modern, inclusive political system does not benefit those who profit from corruption.

Another argument suggests that the international community will contribute to a troubled country's economic development and assistance only after the local government decides to govern properly. "Don't get me wrong. I believe change is possible and am ready to invest in it. But it has got to start with them wanting it," Thomas Freidman wrote. "But we must stop wanting good government more than they do."[7]

However, how should "they" be defined? The people of Somalia want good governance, but those in power or seeking power do not. Good governance entails accountability and compromise, not traits associated with a corrupt and unelected government. Both developed and developing countries need inclusive political institutions and inclusive economics where the people and elite share power and resources.[8] When the state comprised of those elite few takes the resources and benefits of the nation for itself, it divorces its interests from those of the people. "The people who suffer from the extractive institutions cannot hope for absolutist rulers to voluntarily change political institutions and redistribute power in society," Daron Acemoglu and Jams Robinson wrote in *Why Nations Fail:* "The only way to change these political institutions is to force the elite to create more pluralist institutions."[9] A country with enough people focused on obtaining their common interests will force the elite to change.

A brief example demonstrates national unity's influence. In contrast to the failed intervention in Somalia is the 2000 international mission in East Timor. For the first time since World War II, an international body, acting through an appointed administrator took total control of all of the instruments of a national sovereignty. United Nations Transitional Administration in East Timor (UNTAET) ran everything from the power stations and fire departments to radio, television, and U.N. newspaper.[10] The UNTAET

70

mission was successful, in part because the mission was organized around a lead nation, in this case Australia, the Indonesian–occupiers acquiesced and the East Timorese wanted the UN's mission to succeed.

The East Timorese and regional powers supported UNTAET's mission. "We were given Mission Possible," says Peter Galbraith, a former U.S. ambassador to Croatia, who was in charge of political affairs in UNTAET from January 2000 until the summer of 2001. "The mission was completely congruent with people's wishes. We had adequate security resources. No countries opposed Timorese independence, including Indonesia. There was no equivalent of Serbia. The Timorese had good leaders and Sergio's diplomacy was superb."[11] This unity of effort and purpose in the host nation allows for the success of international intervention.

Fostering Compromise from the Outside?

In a larger sense, Somalia represents the limits of international intervention to solve the underlying political problems of a troubled nation. We could give every Somali a cell phone or camel or food for a year, but without an overwhelming desire for peace and reconciliation, the Somalis soon will consume the aid or warlords would steal it with little lasting benefit. The international community could take over the Somali government by establishing an international administration or the UN could broaden AMISOM's mission to include nation building and disarmament. The international community could train Somali officials on proper governance and install inspectors to audit their books to ensure the government properly spent the aid. But with Somali's fierce independence, history of resistance to foreign intrusion and skilled practice at corruption, these efforts will only bear short-term results.

71

As many commentators have stated, a Somali led peace process and Somali formed solutions will work best. Of course, few would dispute this perscription. But what does this concept mean in practical terms, especially in a country with such strategic importance and whose warlords grasp power so fiercely? Forced negotiation and economic aid alone will not succeed. Since the international community began holding conferences to establish a solution for Somalia, the focus concerned creation of a central government by "brokering power sharing deals" rather than democratic representation.[12] Spreading aid around to local communities in order to build a middle class will not work either without accompanying political reform, because democracy means more than economic prosperity. "Nobody is going to give Africa enough aid to buy democracy, and democracy cannot be bought," Claude Ake wrote. "It has to be won in struggle in a world in which people do not voluntarily give up power or treat the economic and political aspects of their lives as discrete entities."[13]

In addition to ownership of the peace process Somalis need to lead the process, because they understand the intricacies of their society, something that outsiders understand barely, if at all. Former Ambassador to Ethiopia, David Shinn, witnessed several internationally sponsored Somali peace conferences and recommends that any future peace conferences have no foreign participation and take place in Somalia. Foreigners stand in the way of progress, Shinn wrote:

> During negotiations in which foreigners play a role, Somalis have developed to a level I have encountered nowhere else in Africa the ability to tell foreigners, with a completely straight face, what they want them to hear or what they think they should hear. I can probably count on one hand the number of foreigners who even appreciate the magnitude of this challenge.[14]

What would a Somali-led process look like? President Yoweri Museveni of Uganda, whose nation contributes the majority of forces to the AMISOM mission, believes that participating in the global market and democratic elections will help create peace. "A modern life requires specialization and exchange of products," Museveni said. "We, therefore, need markets and integration to create those markets in a continent that was Balkanized by colonialism."[15] Along with exchange of products, elected democratic government will decrease conflict. "The need to establish an accountable government has the possibility of forcing factions (sectarian and otherwise) to work together because no single clan can win national power by itself through a democratic election. Democracy, in whatever form, forces groups to seek for alliances. To be a warlord, you do not need internal alliances. You can be a warlord by solely depending on external sponsors."[16]

The warlords and leaders of Al-Shabaab will not give up power easily; however, with AMISOM's success and people's frustration with the last 20 years perhaps rule by the gun has ended and traditional peace-building measures will have room to function. The Somali doctor and humanitarian Dr. Hawa Adbi said, "If Al-Shabaab leave, as [is] the Somali habit we will go and sit under the trees, we will talk about the region, among the clans, and the problem will be solved. Only the Somalis can do it, but with economic support."[17]

International Economic Support

The international community provided Somalia with billions in support these last 20 years. Many nations may ask why should we support Somalia any longer given the country's track record of misappropriating aid? Why should taxpayers allow their hard earned income to go towards assisting a country that steals aid when people at home need assistance? The international community should rationalize and ensure transparency in how the Somali government spends aid. The UN already controls Somali airspace; perhaps it could increase supervision over monies received from national assets and provide greater oversight over international aid as envisioned by discussions at the United Kingdom's international Conference on Somalia in London in February 2012.

The International Civil Aviation Organization of the United Nations took over Somali airspace in 1996. The organization has faced criticism from Somalis since it collects over-flight fees for planes flying through Somali airspace, but little of the money reaches Somalia. The Agency controls Somali airspace from Nairobi, Kenya and collects around $4 million a year from air navigation charges, most of which goes towards administrative costs.[18] If the administration could be made more cost-effective and efficient, similar oversight could be placed over the ports in Mogadishu and eventually Kismayo once Al-Shabaab falls there, so that all Somalis receive the benefit of taxes and duties created by the ports.

The Final Communiqué from the London Conference endorses the establishment of the Joint Financial Management Board that aims to eliminate corruption and maximize use of Somalia's national assets. The impetus for the Board began in September 2011 when the East African Community (EAC) and the Inter-Governmental Authority on Development (IGAD) declared that a joint donor financial management should be created "to manage all financial resources provided to the TFG from both internal and external sources."[19] Initial members of the Board include: the TFG, the United Kingdom, the French Republic, the European Union; and the World Bank. The Board will administer a wide mandate to include management of international revenue from national assets and foreign donations. It aims to provide transparency and promote strong Somali public finance institutions.[20]

The international community could also assist by supporting programs that develop civil society, such as women's groups and moderate Islamic organizations like Ahlu Sunna Waljama (ASWJ). Promotion of Somali businesses through resources from the Joint Financial Board would bind the government to the people through the creation of a broader business class. Many businessmen support Al-Shabaab and view the current dysfunction as being better than the alternative of a strong, predatory government that imposes high taxes with nothing in return.

No quick solution of giving massive amounts of aid to the central government for distribution or funding large developmental projects will make a lasting difference. These larger projects place the international community or the U.S. as power brokers or participants in governing, rather than as a supporter. The Joint Financial Board as currently conceived will have much authority, but the amount of aid and tax dollars wasted by the transitional government requires the Board to have a broad mandate in the hope of increasing the ability of the Somali public to benefit.

The Role of the U.S. Government

U.S. policy, outside of counter-terrorism and antipiracy actions, should also focus on small, incremental, limited assistance. This assistance should focus on emergency humanitarian aid, small business assistance, agricultural improvements and environmental programs. These programs should strive to improve the lives of Somalis while they build civil society. The programs should not be large enough to invite conflict over aid or impose an American face. In addition, the programs should be small enough so as not to impose the U.S. as a substantial player in tilting the balance of power significantly one way or another between clans or other rivals. All of the agencies in the government have a role in a limited approach aimed at supporting civil organizations.

The U.S. military or AMISOM forces could support training missions and building local capacity. These missions would focus on foreign internal defense. If needed for humanitarian reasons, a limited armed intervention like Operation Restore Hope could be conducted that provides security for aid but ends before conducting stabilization efforts.

Economically, the U.S. could assist in seizing assets of those enriched through corruption. More importantly, the U.S. should support trade with Somali business. Establishing ties between the United States Chamber of Commerce and Somali businessmen would create more stability than another internationally sponsored peace conference; "Somalia needs a Chamber of Commerce before it needs a cabinet."[21]

Diplomatically, our best effort may be to keep a low profile. We should support the efforts of non-governmental organizations and international organizations so as not to place an American face on peace-building or government-building efforts. We should support and interact with women's groups, locally run aid organizations and moderate religious groups, while using diplomatic pressure to ostracize spoilers to peace building.

Conclusion

The international community and the U.S. should provide support around the edges of Somali politics and society. Actively engaging the center through a brokered peace deal or lengthy military occupation invites corruption and mistrust. Aggressive intervention such as establishing an international administration over Somalia would unnecessarily cause friction. It also would delay Somalia's development as a unified, strong country. Numerous Somalis possess the technical ability to run a government. What is missing is accountability. As business people, religious leaders, clan elders, local governments, women's groups and local non-governmental agencies spread and strengthen, they will stand as counterweights to Somalia's historically predatory central government. Their organizations will demand compromises with each other and with the government. As civil society stands up Somalis will make peace themselves and we should support the peacemakers.

---

[1]Daron Acemoglu and Jams Robinson, *Why Nations Fail: The Origins of Power, Prosperity, and Poverty* (New York: Crown Business, 2012), 68.

[2]Ioan Lewis, *Understanding Somalia and Somaliland* (New York: Columbia University Press, 2008), 91.

[3]Richard J. Norton, "Somalia II," http://www.au.af.mil/au/awc/awcgate/navy/pmi/somalia2.pdf (accessed 2 March 2012).

[4]Michael A. Weinstein, "The Root Cause of Somalia Political Conflicts," *Garowe Online*, 13 April 2010, http://www.garoweonline.com/artman2/publish/Features_34/Dr_Weinstein_The_Root_Cause_of_Somalia_Political_Conflicts.shtml (accessed 28 March 2012).

[5]Mark Bowden, *Black Hawk Down: A Story of Modern War* (New York: Penguin Books, 1999), 335.

[6]Fareed Zakaria, "Fantasy and Reality in Afghanistan," *Washington Post*, 29 February 2012.

[7]Thomas L. Freidman, "A Festival of Lies," *The New York Times*, 24 March 2012.

[8]See Acemoglu and Robinson, 65.

[9]Ibid., 86-87.

[10]Jonathan Steele, "Nation Building in East Timor," *World Policy Journal* 19, no. 2 (Summer 2002): 78.

[11]Ibid.

[12]Accord, 18.

[13]Ake, 173.

[14]David Shinn, "Al-Shabaab and Somalia in the 21st Century," 25 January 2012, Remarks at Interagency Workshop on External Support to Al-Shabaab Organized by Navanti Group, New York City, http://davidshinn.blogspot.com/ 2012/01/al-shabaab-and-somalia.html (accessed 14 March 2012).

[15]Yoweri Museveni, "Uganda: Somalia Solution Lies in Three-Tier Approach," Transcript of Remarks by the President of Uganda to the Somalia London Confernce, AllAfrica, 24 February 2012, http://allafrica.com/stories/201202271703.html (accessed 2 March 2012).

[16]Ibid.

[17]Clar Ni Chonghaile, "Somali Doctor: 'They are Taking my Land so I Can't Welcome the Poor," *The Guardian,* 14 March 2012.

[182]Jeffrey Gettlemen, "Somalia Wobbly on Ground, Seeks Control of Its Airspace," *The New York Times,* 14 April 2011.

[19]Foreign and Commonwealth Office of the UK, "London Conference on Somalia: Communique, Annex A: Declaration by the Initial Members of the Joint Financial Management Board at the London Conference," 23 Februray 2012, http://www.fco.gov.uk/resources/en/pdf/global-issues/731221182/communique-annexa (accessed 19 March 2012).

[20]Ibid.

[21]Alex De Waal, "Getting Somalia Right This Time," *The New York Times*, 21 February 2012.

BIBLIOGRAPHY

Books

Acemoglu, Daron, and Jams Robinson. *Why Nations Fail: The Origins of Power, Prosperity, and Poverty.* New York: Crown Business, 2012.

Ake, Claude. *The Feasibility of Democracy in Africa.* Dakar, Sengal: Council for the Development of Social Science Research in Africa, 2000.

Baumann, Robert, Lawrence Yates, and Versalle Washington. *My Clan Against the World: US and Coalition Forces in Somalia 1992-1994.* Ft. Leavenworth, KS: Combat Studies Institute Press, 2004.

Bowden, Mark. *Black Hawk Down: A Story of Modern War*. New York: Penguin Books, 1999.

Bradbury, Mark. *Becoming Somaliland.* London: Progressio, 2008.

Cassanelli, Lee V. *The Shaping of Somali Society: Reconstructing the History of a Pastoral People, 1600-1900.* Philadelphia, PA: University of Pennsylvania Press, 1982.

Elmi, Afyare Abdi. *Understanding the Somalia Conflagration–Identity, Political Islam and Peacebuilding.* London: Pluto Press, 2010.

Harper, Mary. *Getting Somalia Wrong? Faith, War and Hope in a Shattered State.* London: Zed Book, 2012.

Issa-Salwe, Abdisalam. *The Collapse of the Somali State: The Impact of the Colonial Legacy.* London: Haan Publishing, 1996.

Laitin, David D., and Said S. Samatar. *Somalia: Nation in Search of State.* Boulder, CO: Westview Press, 1987.

Lewis, Ioan. *Understanding Somalia and Somaliland.* New York: Columbia University Press, 2008.

Power, Samantha. *A Problem from Hell: America and the Age of Genocide.* New York: Basis Books, 2002.

Shultz, Richard H. Jr., and Andrea J. Dew. *Insurgents, Terrorists and Militias: The Warriors of Contemporary Combat.* New York: Columbia University Press, 2006.

Government Documents

Council on Foreign Relations. "Somalia's Clan Families and Major Sub-Clans" 2002. http://www.cfr.org/somalia/somalias-clan-families/p13315 (accessed 2 May 2012).

Dagne, Ted. *Somalia: Current Conditions and Prospects for a Lasting Peace.* 8 October 2010. 7-5700.

Swan, James C. "Speech by the U.S. Special Representative for Somalia Ambassador." Ohio State University, 9 November 2011.

United Nations.Office for the Coordination of Humanitarian Affairs. *Consolidated Appeal Process, Somalia 2012.* December 2011.

_____. S/2007/436. *Report of the Monitoring Group on Somalia Pursuant to Security Council Resolution 1724 (2006).* 27 June 2007.

_____. S/2008/769. *Report of the Monitoring Group on Somalia Pursuant to Security Council Resolution 1724 (2008).* 20 November 2008.

_____. S/2011/433. *Report of the Monitoring Group on Somalia and Eritrea pursuant to Security Council Resolution 1916 (2010).* 18 July 2011.

_____. A/66/657-S/2012/33. *Report of the Secretary-General. Conflict-Related Sexual Violence.* 13 January 2012.

_____. *Special Report of the Secretary-General on Somalia.* 31 January 2012.

United Nations Security Council. S/2011/549. *Report of the Secretary-General on Somalia.* 30 August 2011.

_____. S/2011/759. *Report of the Secretary General on Somalia.* 9 December 2011.

_____. *United Nations Security Council Resolution 814.* 26 March 1993.

_____. *United Nations Security Council Resolution 2036.* 22 February 2012.

U.S. House of Representatives. Committee on Foreign Affairs. *Deputy Assistant Secretary Reuben Brigety, II, Bureau of Population, Refugees, and Migration, U.S. Department of State, Assessing the Consequences of the Failed State of Somalia: Hearing before the Subcommittee on Africa, Global Health and Human rights and the Subcommittee on Terrorism, Nonproliferation and Trade,* July 2011.

_____. Committee on Foreign Affairs. *Prepared Remarks of Bronwyn Bruton Fellow, One Earth Future Foundation, Assessing the Consequences of the Failed State of*

Somalia: Hearing before the Subcommittee on Africa, Global Health and Human Rights and the Subcommittee on Terrorism, Nonproliferation and Trade, 7 July 2011.

_____. Committee on Foreign Affairs. *Prepared Remarks of Dr. J. Peter Pham, Assessing the Consequences of the Failed State of Somalia: Hearing before the Subcommittee on Africa, Global Health and Human Rights and the Subcommittee on Terrorism, Nonproliferation and Trade,* 7 July 2011.

U.S. President. "Presidential Study Directive on Mass Atrocities," Presidential Study Directive, PSD-10." 4 August 2011.

U.S. Senate. Committee on Foreign Relations. *Testimony of Assistant Secretary Johnnie Carson, Bureau of African Affairs, U.S. Department of State, "Developing a Coordinated and Sustainable U.S. Strategy Toward Somalia: Hearing before the Subcommittee on African Affairs,* 20 May 2009.

_____. *Unclassified Statement for the Record, James R. Clapper, Director of National Intelligence on the Worldwide Threat,"Assessment of the US Intelligence Community: Testimony before the Select Committee on Intelligence,* 31 January 2012.

<u>Internet Sources</u>

"Africa: Resolving Conflicts Remains a Top U.S. Policy Priority, Carson Says." *All Africa,* 12 March 2012. http://allafrica.com/stories/201203131400.html (accessed 26 March 2012).

African Development Bank. "African Development Fund. Somalia Country Brief." February 2010. http://www.afdb.org/fileadmin/uploads/afdb/Documents/Project-and-Operations/SOMALIA%20-%20Country%20Brief.pdf (accessed 28 March 2012).

Ahmed, Mohammed Daoud. "Solving the Somali Jigsaw." *Think Africa Press,* 7 March 2012. http://thinkafricapress.com/somalia/somali-jigsaw (accessed 13 April 2012).

Bahadur, Jay. "TFG Corruption: An Exclusive Report. Part I: The Cash Kleptocracy." *Somalia Report*, 21 February 2012. http://www.somaliareport.com/index.php/post/2855/TFG_Corruption_An_Exclusive_Report (accessed 27 March 2012).

_____. "TFG Corruption: An Exclusive Report. Part II: Of Budgets and Briefcase Ministries." *Somalia Report,* 27 February 2012. http://somaliareport.com/index.php/post/2938/TFG_Corruption_An_Exclusive_Report///. (accessed 29 March 2012).

Baugh, Matt. "London Conference on Somalia: Political Process." http://blogs.fco.gov. uk/mattbaugh/ (accessed 8 February 2012).

BBC News. "Who Runs Somalia?" http://www.bbc.co.uk/news/world-africa (accessed 11 April 2012).

Bryden, Matt. "Somalia's Famine is Not Just a Catastrophe, It's a Crime." October 2011. http://www.enoughproject.org/files/Bryden_SomaliaFamine%20 Brief_final_0.pdf (accessed 3 May 2012).

Cadde, Aweys. "Galmudug Demands Clans Hand Over Weapons." *Somalia Report,* 20 March 2012. http://www.somaliareport.com/index.php/post/3111 (accessed 14 April 2012).

Central Intelligence Agency. "World Factbook. Somalia. Economy." https://www.cia. gov/library/publications/the-world-factbook/geos/so.html (accessed 30 January 2012).

Center for Strategic and International Studies. "The Dadaab Refugee Complex: A Powder Keg and It's Giving Off Sparks." http://csis.org/print/35548. (accessed 19 April 2012).

Gundel, Joakim. "The Predicament of 'Oday:' The Role of Traditional Structures in Security, Right, Law and Development in Somalia." Danish Refugee Council & Novib/Oxfam, 8 November 2006. http://www.logcluster.org/ops/som/ infrastructurecommunicationvarious/Gundel_The%20role%20of%20traditional% 20structures.pdf (accessed 30 March 2012).

Erdogan, Recep Tayyip. "The Tears of Somalia." *Foreign Policy,* 10 October 2011. http://www.foreignpolicy.com/articles/2011/10/10/the_tears_of_somalia?showco mments=yes (accessed 7 December 2011).

Eubank, Nicholas. "Taxation, Political Accountability, and Foreign Aid: Lessons from Somaliland." *Journal of Development Studies,* 26 March 2011. http://ssrn.com/ abstract=1621374. (accessed 26 March 2012).

Evans, Garath. "End of the Argument–How We Won the Debate to Stop Genocide." *Foreign Policy*, December 2011. http://www.foreignpolicy.com/articles/ 2011/11/28gareth_evans_end_of_the_argument (accessed 10 February 2012).

Fartagg, Abdirazak. "Audit Investigative Report–2011: Transitional Federal Government, Somalia," 20 February 2012. http://somaliareport.com/downloads/Audit_ Investigative_Report___2011_Consolidatedx.pdf. (accessed 27 March 2012).

Foreign and Commonwealth Office of the UK. London Conference on Somalia. "Communique, Annex A: Declaration by the Initial Members of the Joint Financial Management Board at the London Conference." 23 February 2012.

http://www.fco.gov.uk/resources/en/pdf/global-issues/731221182/communique-annexa (accessed 19 March 2012).

Forestry Department. "Global Forest Resources Assessment 2010. Country Report–Somalia." FRA2010/194. 2010. http://www.fao.org/docrep/013/al629E/al629e.pdf. (accessed 16 April 2012).

Genocide Watch: The International Alliance to End Genocide. "Mass Atrocities Alert: Somalia." March 2012. http://www.genocidewatch.org/somalia.html (accessed 5 April 2012).

Gettleman, Jeffrey. "The Most Dangerous Place in the World." *Foreign Policy*, 16 February 2009. http://www.foreignpolicy.com/articles/2009/02/16/the_most_dangerous_place_in_the_world? (accessed 10 January 2012).

Griswold, Eliza. "Hawa Abdi, Doctor; Human-Rights Activist." *The Atlantic,* November 2011. http://www.theatlantic.com/magazine/archive/2011/11/hawa-abdi/8664 (accessed 10 December 2011).

Hassan, Sayyid Mohammed Abdile (the Mad Mullah). "Camel Milk a Source of Sustenance for Somalis." Translated by Ahmed Ali Abokor. *Wardheer News,* 29 August 2009. http://wardheernews.com/Articles_09/Aug/29_camel_milk_faisal.html. (accessed 11 April 2012).

Hersi, Ali Abdi. "Continuing Governance Crisis in Somalia: The Bitter Fruit of the Somali's Faulty Approach to the Practice of Statehood." *Wardheer News,* 26 June 2006. http://www.wardheernews.com/Articles_06/june_06/26_Somalia_Governance.Crisis_Dr.A.Hirsi2.html (accessed 3 April 2012).

Hornlighter. "Interview with Degan Ali, Executive Director of Horn Relief." 2 February 2012. http://hornlight.org/2012/02/interview-with-degan-ali-executive-director-of-horn-relief/ (accessed 19 April 2012).

Integrated Regional Information Networks: Humanitarian News and Analysis. "Somalia: Burkas to Tracksuits." 17 April 2012. http://www.irinnews.org/report/95308/SOMALIA-Burkas-to-tracksuits. (accessed 19 April 2012).

Kantai, Parselelo. "Inside Garissa Lodgo, Nairobi's Somali Trading Hub." *The Africa Report*, 31 January 2011. http://www.theafricareport.com/index.php/east-horn-africa/inside-garissa-lodge-nairobi-s-somali-trading-hub-5136196.html (accessed 24 March 2012).

Kantai, Parselelo, and Patrick Smith. "The Dangers of Carving Up Somalia." *The Africa Report*, 6 February 2011. http://www.theafricareport.com/index.php/news-analysis/the-dangers-of-carving-up-somalia-50180834.html (accessed 10 March 2012).

Mire, Sucaad. "Somalia's Nobel Peace Prize Nominee." *Somalia Report*, 24 March 2012. http://www.somaliareport.com/index.php/post/3140/Somalias_Nobel_Peace_Priz e_Nominee. (accesed 19 April 2012).

Mubarak. "Mubarak's Musings, Somalia's Roadmap to Peace or War?" *Somalia Report,* 2 May 2012. http://www.somaliareport.com/index.php/post/3306/Mubaraks_ Musings (accessed 3 May 2012).

Museveni, Yoweri. "Uganda: Somalia Solution Lies in Three-Tier Approach." Transcript of Remarks by the President of Uganda to the Somalia London Conference on 24 February 2012. AllAfrica. http://allafrica.com/stories/201202271703.html (accessed 2 March 2012).

Norris, John, and Bronwyn Burton. "The Price of Somalia's Failure, How Much Has the Collapse of Somalia Cost the World?" *Foreign Policy*, 5 October 2011. http://www.foreignpolicy.com/articles/2011/10/05/the_price_of_failure? (accessed 15 December 2011).

Norton, Richard J. "Somalia II." http://www.au.af.mil/au/awc/awcgate/navy/pmi/ somalia2.pdf (accessed 2 March 2012).

Shinn, David. "Al-Shabaab and Somalia in the 21st Century." 25 January 2012. Remarks at Interagency Workshop on External Support to Al-Shabaab, Organized by Navanti Group, New York City. http://davidshinn.blogspot.com/2012/01/al- ,shabaab-and-somalia.html (accessed 14 March 2012).

Somalia National Conference. "Communique from Garowe Second Somali National Consultative Constitutional Conference." 17 February 2012. http://www. raxanreeb.com/2012/02/somalia-communique-from-garowe-second-somali- national-consultative-constitutional-conference/. (accessed 30 March 2012).

Somali Republic. "Somali Transitional Charter, Transitional Federal Charter for the Somali Republic." http://www.unhcr.org/refworld/country,,,LEGISLATION, SOM,456d621e2,4795c2d22,0.html (accessed 28 March 2012).

Transparency International. "Corruption Perceptions Index for 2007-2011." http://www.transparency.org/policy_research/surveys_indices/cpi. (accessed 13 February 2012).

United Nations Department of Field Support. "Map of Somalia." December 2011. http://www.un.org/depts/Cartographic/map/profile/somalia.pdf (accessed 2 May 2012).

United Nations High Commission for Refugees. "Refugees in the Horn of Africa: Somali Displacement Crisis." 2012. http://data.unhcr.org/horn-of-africa/regional.php (accessed 11 May 2012).

_____. "UNCHR Country Operations Profile–Kenya." 2012. http://www.unhcr.org/pages/49e483a16.html (accessed 11 May 2012).

United Nations. "Somalia Country Profile." http://data.un.org/CountryProfile.aspx?crName=Somalia (accessed 30 January 2012).

United Nations Educational, Scientific and Cultural Organization (UNESCO). "Statistics in Brief Eduation Profile Somalia." 2009. http://stats.uis.unesco.org/unesco/TableViewer/document.aspx?ReportId=121&IF_Language=en&BR_Country=7060. (accessed 16 April 2012.)

US Department of State. "Background Note: Somalia." http://www.state.gov/r/pa/ei/bgn/2863.htm#gov. (accessed 29 March 2012).

US Department of Treasury Office of Foreign Assets Control. "Terrorism: What You Need to Know about U.S. Sanctions." http://www.treasury.gov/resource-center/sanctions/Programs/Documents/terror.pdf. (accessed 2 April 2012).

Weinstein, Michael A. "The Root Cause of Somalia Political Conflicts." *Garowe Online*, 13 April 2010. http://www.garoweonline.com/artman2/publish/Features_34/Dr_Weinstein_The_Root_Cause_of_Somalia_Political_Conflicts.shtml (accessed 28 March 2012).

<u>Journals/Periodicals</u>

Bradbury, Mark, and Sally Healy. "Endless War: A Brief History of the Somali Conflict." Accord 21: *Whose Peace Is It Anyway? Connecting Somali and International Peacemaking* (2010): 10.

_____. "Business as Usual, Bakaaro Market in War." In *Accord 21: Whose Peace Is It Anyway? Connecting Somali and International Peacemaking* , edited by Mark Bradbury and Sally Healy. London: Consiliation Resources, 2010: 68.

Grobbelaar, Janis, and Jama Ghalib. "Security and Reconciliation in Post-Conflict Society: The Matter of Closing the Books in South Africa and Somalia." *Bildhaan: An International Journal of Somali Studies* 7, no. 5 (2007): 9.

Mohamed, Jama. "Kinship and Contract in Somali Politics." *Africa* 77, no. 2 (2007): 226-249.

Samatar, Ahmed I. "The Porcupine Dilemma: Governance and Transition in Somalia." *Bildhaan: An International Journal of Somali Studies* 7, no. 6 (2007): 58, 69.

Samatar, Said S. "The Politics of Poetry." *Africa Report* 38, no. 5 (September/October 1993): 16.

Steele, Jonathan. "Nation Building in East Timor." *World Policy Journal* 19, no. 2 (Summer 2002): 78

<u>Newspapers</u>

AAP-Reuter. "Somalia to Break U.K. Relations." *The Sydney Morning Herald*, 12 March 1963.

Apple, R. W. "Somalia: Turmoil in a Land of Proud and Hostile Clans." *New York Times*, 26 October 1969.

Chonghaile, Clar Ni. "Somali doctor: 'They are Taking my Land so I Can't Welcome the Poor.'" *The Guardian,* 14 March 2012.

Cooper, Helene, Steven Less Myers, and Steven Lee. "U.S. Tactics in Libya May Be a Model for Other Efforts." *The New York Times*, 28 August 2011.

De Waal, Alex. "Getting Somalia Right This Time." *The New York Times*, 21 February 2012.

Editorial. "Now What for Somalia?" *Milwaukee Journal*, 6 July 1960.

Farah, Nuruddin. "My Life as a Diplomat." *The New York Times*, 26 May 2007.

Freidman, Thomas L. "A Festival of Lies." *The New York Times*, 24 March 2012.

Gettlemen, Jeffrey. "Ethiopia Hits Somali Targets, Declaring War." *The New York Times*, 25 December 2006.

_____. "Ethiopian Troops Said to Enter Somalia, Opening New Front Against Militants." *The New York Times*, 21 November 2011.

_____. "For Somali Women, Pain of Being a Spoil of War." *The New York Times,* 27 December 2011.

_____. "A Killing Strains Somalia's Hold on its Tenuous Peace." *New York Times*, 29 July 2006.

_____. "Somalis Say Ethiopian Presence is Just the Uniforms." *The New York Times,* 22 July 2006.

_____. "Somalia Wobbly on Ground, Seeks Control of Its Airspace." *The New York Times,* 14 April 2011.

_____. "A Taste of Hope in Somalia's Battered Capital." *The New York Times,* 3 April 2012.

Gismatullin, Eduard. "Vancouver-based Africa Oil Defies Al-Qaeda in Billion-barrel Somali Well Drill." *The Vancouver Sun,* 5 March 2012.

Jones, Rachel Pieh. "A Child of Two Worlds." *The New York Times*, 23 February 2012.

Maasho, Aaron. "Ethiopian Troops Set to Leave Somalia by End of April: AU." *Somaliland Sun,* 11 March 2012.

MacFarquhar, Neil. "At U.N., Pressure Is on Russia for Refusal to Condemn Syria." *The New York Times*, 31 January 2012.

Mutiga, Murithi. "Modgadishu Rumbles Back to Life as the Shabaab Falters." *The Daily Nation,* 3 March 2012.

Odula, Tom. "Eritrea: We Can't Supply Somali Militants Weapons." *Associated Press*, 11 November 2011.

_____. "Somalia's Children Schooled in Guns." *Washington Times,* 14 March 2012.

Rosenburg, Tina. "In Famine, Vouchers Can Be Tickets to Survival." *The New York Times,* 27 October 2011.

Shanker, Thom and Eric Schmitt. "Seeing Limits to 'New' Kind of War in Libya." *The New York Times*, 21 October 2011.

Shannon, Lisa. "The Rape of Somalia's Women Is Being Ignored." *The Guardian,* 11 October 2011.

"Somalia–A Dry Hungry Land Manages to Survive." *New York Times*, 31 January 1966.

Walz, Jay. "Somalia Facing Grave Problems." *New York Times*, 5 July 1960.

Zakaria, Fareed. "Fantasy and Reality in Afghanistan." *Washington Post,* 29 February 2012.

Reports

International Crisis Group. *The Kenyan Military Intervention in Somalia. Africa Report Number 184.* New York: International Crisis Group, 15 February 2012.

Megisteab, Kidane. "Critical Factors in the Horn of Africa's Raging Conflicts." Discussion Paper 67, *Nordiska Afrikainstitutet*, 2011.

Nenova, Tatiana, and Tim Harford. "Anarchy and Invention: How Does Somalia's Private Sector Cope without Government." *Public Policy for the Private Sector.* Washington, DC: World Bank, November 2004.

Norris, John, and Bronwyn Bruton. *Twenty Years of Collapse and Counting: The Cost of Failure in Somalia.* Washington, DC: Center for American Progress and One Earth Future Foundation, September 2011.

Poole, Walter S. "The Effort to Save Somalia: August 1992-March 1994." Washington, DC: Government Printing Office, 2005.